Mother of the Universe

Mother of the Universe

"These magnificently profound, expanding, and expansive recreations of Ramprasad by Lex Hixon not only bring to us some of the wildest and most far-reaching insights into the nature of Indian civilization and the Mother and thousands of years of devotion, but also speak, sometimes unnervingly and always extremely impassionedly, right to the heart of all seekers of the truth in this burning and terribly menaced world. No one who wants to approach and enjoy the mystery of the Divine Feminine in its paradoxical glory should be without this book."

    Andrew Harvey, author of *Hidden Journey, Journey in Ladakh,* and
    coauthor of *Dialogues with a Modern Mystic*

"Lex Hixon's *Mother of the Universe* brings Kali's dance to us in a fluid, living way that engages our whole self and awakens us to the cosmic within us. To open to the Goddess Kali through Hixon and Ramprasad is to call ourselves forth into the ultimate reality of embracing the mystery, the unknown, and the unexpected. Ramprasad's devotion is total, and through Hixon's rewritings, we are beckoned to find the Divine Mother's conscious core of love and wisdom that brings meaning to our lives in a time of drastic change. Her unconditional love remains a paradox only when we cling to the status quo and exterior criteria of reality.

    Kali's nonlinear tradition moves in mysterious ways in the world. I recommend reading Ramprasad's poems on a daily basis. Through a daily absorption, the terror of the luminous darkness can be blissfully embraced, enabling all other fears to be nullified. These poems are translucent vessels of divine energy pouring out the nectar-medicine that can transmute the world's poison."

    Rowena Pattee Kryder, author of *The Gaia Matrix Oracle* and
    The Faces of the Moon Mother

"A brilliant, luminous, free, and fiery rendition of Ramprasad's verses of the Goddess. Not the 'Goddess' of the ideologues, who want Her to support one postmodern position against another, but rather the true Goddess as the Ground of all positions, high or low, sacred or profane—the primordial enlightened mind that embraces the entire Kosmos with care and concern, ecstatic love and fierce compassion, the water in which all fishes equally swim, the water that is our own source, suchness, essence, being, and blessing.

    As always, Lex's renditions are a direct transmission of the Living Truth, known by many names, and most beautifully in this case, as our divine and dearest Mother. Partake of these verses, partake of the Goddess. The reader is the actual subject of these verses; the Goddess is the one doing the reading, smiling gently to Herself, and remembering just what She did to merit such surprise."

    Ken Wilber, author of *The Spectrum of Consciousness, The Atman Project,* and *Grace & Grit*

Mother of the Universe

Visions of the Goddess and Tantric Hymns of Enlightenment

Lex Hixon

QUEST BOOKS
The Theosophical Publishing House

Wheaton, IL U.S.A./Madras, India/London, England

The Theosophical Publishing House
P.O. Box 270
Wheaton, IL 60189-0270

A publication of the Theosophical Publishing House,
a department of the Theosophical Society in America

*This publication made possible with
the assistance of the Kern Foundation*

Library of Congress Cataloging–in–Publication Data

Hixon, Lex.
    Mother of the Universe / Lex Hixon.
        p.   cm.
    Selected from Jadunath Sinha's Rama Prasada's devotional songs
    ISBN 0–8356–0702–X : $16.00
    1. Kali (Hindu deity)—Poetry. I. Lex, Hixon. II. Sinha,
Jadunath, 1894–   Rama Prasada's devotional songs. III. Title.
PK1718.R2514A25   1994
811' .54—dc20
                                                            94–6146
                                                               CIP

9 8 7 6 5 4 3 2 1 * 94 95 96 97 98 99

Printed in the United States of America by Versa Press

DEDICATION

These hymns of enlightenment are dedicated to lovers of radical truth everywhere, especially those attracted by the blissful Goddess. This volume is offered at the feet of my spiritual parents, Ramakrishna Paramahamsa and Sarada Devi of Bengal, and the stream of illumined souls flowing from their powerful transmission of Kali Wisdom—women and men who now manifest freely and joyfully within all sacred traditions on the planet, dissolving limits, crossing over boundaries, unveiling harmony and omniconscious unity for all beings.

Shanti! Shanti! Shanti!

CONTENTS

CONTEMPORARY VISIONS OF THE GODDESS

PREFACE

*I*n 1966, I received initiation into the Divine Mother tradition of India, as practiced by the extraordinary adepts of Mother Wisdom, Ramakrishna Paramahamsa and Sarada Devi, who lived in nineteenth-century Bengal. I was attracted to this radiant couple by an amazing document, *The Gospel of Sri Ramakrishna,* first published in English in 1942. Here I first encountered God, or Ultimate Reality, addressed and experienced as Mother. Having been raised in the environment of Jewish-Christian culture, where the root metaphor for approaching the Divine is masculine, my immediate response was surprised delight at the naturalness and evident power of the feminine metaphor.

Almost thirty years ago, when I was in my early twenties, the seed of Ramakrishna's mystical intimacy with the Mother of the Universe was transmitted to me in the traditional Hindu ceremony of initiation, conducted by Swami Nikhilananda, a direct disciple of Sarada Devi, the fully enlightened wife and powerful successor of Ramakrishna. Embraced within this fresh, vibrant lineage of spiritual transmission, I was presented directly with the Wisdom Goddess and with modes of contemplation most suited to appreciating and communing with her. Now I can approach and envision the Great Goddess naturally, as if I had been raised since childhood in the Divine Mother tradition of Bengal, which centers around the beautiful black Warrior of Wisdom, the sword-bearing Kali of the noble Tantra—not destructive and dark, but blissful and brilliant.

I retain a Western sensibility about language and meaning, which I have tried to infuse into this book of visionary encounters with

Mother Reality. This may permit the astonishing world of the Goddess to be more accessible and hopefully more inspiring to readers of English worldwide, many of whom live within cultures governed primarily by masculine metaphors for Divinity and by masculine attitudes toward reality.

Authentic acquaintance with this ancient, living stream of Goddess Wisdom will provide much-needed resources for the nontraditional, secular culture called the modern world. Mother Reality remains tender, playful, open, creative, unconventional, and indefinable. She is fundamentally the open space beyond religion, which I call timeless awareness. She stands always outside frameworks. Yet her unitive wisdom also presents a way to harmonize genuine religious and cultural traditions which advance rival claims. Mother loves all her children equally.

What is presented in *Mother of the Universe* are the visionary hymns of Ramprasad Sen from eighteenth-century Bengal. I have not worked from the original Bengali text. Selected from English translations by Jadunath Sinha of the two hundred fifty extant songs of Ramprasad, these one hundred twenty-six expanded versions have gradually unfolded over the last twelve years. The Bengali verses are shorthand, as lyrics always are. My contemplative versions represent an articulated literary form, designed not to be sung but recited aloud, thereby retaining a sense of the oral tradition which these poems represent. Rather than using scholarly footnotes, the expanded poems themselves contain commentary on the esoteric Mother Wisdom of India and, more particularly, on the tantric tradition of Bengal, which has its roots in both Buddhism and Hinduism.

These are spontaneous songs, sung over two hundred years ago by Ramprasad, an intense lover of the Goddess. More than sacred offerings to the Mother of the Universe, these are direct encounters with Mother Reality. Their startling imagery and naked honesty belong to Ramprasad. My expansions have added nothing that diverges from his spirit.

Understood from a deeper perspective, it was the Goddess who sang these revolutionary songs through her precocious child, Ramprasad, in order to awaken the entire world to the teaching of Mother Wisdom—invisible to linear thinking, far beyond theology. The energy of these ecstatic hymns is still enlivening and completely contemporary. Their function continues. As Ramprasad sings to those involved in spiritual cultivation: "If you find farming difficult, please bring my poems with you."

Mother of the Universe presents, through the vivid mode of Goddess worship, the Mother Wisdom which is always unitive, never divisive. These pages do not introduce some philosophical or literary alternative but unveil the living force which exists at the very heart of awareness as the upward flowing power of liberation and illumination called Mother Kundalini. These poems are existential inquiry. They are Goddess energy.

Ramprasad's tantric songs represent the actual experiences of a great adept. They can now be experienced anew by sensitive readers of modern times, not as romantic glimpses into some ancient era or exotic culture but as openings into the global civilization of the near future. By her very nature, Mother is always global, always indivisible, always revolutionary. This book can serve as a nondoctrinal, nonofficial scripture of the Goddess. We can drink deep from Mother Wisdom through the practice of oral recitation. Each song opens unique channels in the subtle body. The poems travel within us as we travel within the poems. There is no repetition here, although there is mutual resemblance and mutual illumination. Each mystic hymn represents a new encounter, a new gift from Mother. As Ramprasad sings: "Dive with abandon into her mystery and discover a new gem every moment."

As scriptural manifestation, these poems deserve concentrated rather than just casual reading. By assimilating one of these visions each day for one hundred twenty-six days, one could make an intimate meditation retreat with the Goddess in the midst of one's daily responsibilities, which is precisely the nonseparative mode of contemplative practice she favors. Ramprasad sings: "Ordinary existence in the heart of the extended family is the supreme worship beyond worship which perceives Mother Reality as every being, every situation, every breath."

Reading aloud, alone or with friends, produces the effect of chanting and permits her teaching to be absorbed more directly by the entire being. With melodious voices, may we welcome Goddess Wisdom to manifest more and more openly at the heart of contemporary world culture—purifying, healing, harmonizing, and enlightening. With Ramprasad, we cry out to everyone her secret mantra, *Ma! Ma! Ma!*

INTRODUCTION
THE NATURE OF MOTHER WISDOM

*O Wisdom Goddess, your essence alone is present
within every life, every event. Your living power
flows freely as this universe. Wherever I go and
wherever I look, I perceive only you, my blissful
Mother, radiating as pure cosmic play.*

Ramprasad

*T*he Great Mother is humanity's most primordial, per-
vasive, and fruitful image of reality. Either secretly or openly, she
appears with extraordinary power, wisdom, and tenderness at the
core of every noble culture. She illuminates the entire universe,
because she is not some local or limited goddess but our Universal
Mother. She expresses herself fluently through and within every
sacred tradition, without needing to call attention to her femi-
nine nature.

Various feminine expressions of the Divine abounded in the
ancient world. The many authentic appearances of Virgin Mary—
at Tepeyac in Mexico, Fatima in Portugal, and Gerabondal in
Spain, Lourdes in France, and contemporary apparitions in Egypt,
Yugoslavia, and America—are special revelations of her reality for
the modern world. Through the Goddess tradition, alive everywhere
on the planet, she guides, protects, terrifies, chastens, heals, liberates,
and illuminates. Her relation as Great Mother to the cosmos and its
innumerable life forms is as tender as her relation with each precious
human soul. It is a relation so intimate as to be free from subject or
object, that is to say, a relationship which is intrinsically mystical.

1

The Goddess always remains the uncompromising Warrior of Truth—not primarily a nurturing mother figure but a Wisdom Mother who educates and liberates, gradually removing all limits. Her teaching is that of indivisible oneness, surprisingly expressed by the diversity of her cosmic dance through countless civilizations and religions.

The Divine Mother is not distinct in essence from the inscrutable Yahweh of Jewish tradition, God the Hidden Father of Christianity, or Allah Most High of Islam, who is beyond all conceptions or descriptions. She is recognized in Mahayana Buddhism as Prajnaparamita, the depth of unthinkability, Mother of all Buddhas. From the radiant blackness of the womb of Mother Reality emerge numerous messengers of truth, profoundly mature women and men who have graced every culture throughout history. Also from her reality emerge cruel and arrogant human beings who create dramas of suffering and conflict that she uses to awaken, purify, and elevate the soul. From her alone flow cosmic harmony and cosmic disaster.

The Goddess tradition appears to exist in its most undiluted practice on the planet today within the ancient tantric lineages of Hinduism and Buddhism, which are being passed on intact, even to the present generation. Some observers note that the majority of teachers and advanced practitioners in these ancient traditions are male. This fact does not present any obstacle to the functioning of Goddess energy, and the balance is rapidly changing, as the largest movement on the planet today is the women's movement. This change is already evident as a great prominence of modern women in the realm of spiritual practice.

The primordial worship of the Great Goddess in the Middle East and Europe is indirectly reflected now as the veneration of the Virgin Mary and the sublime women saints of the Church. But since the Divine Mother is all-pervading, we can find her presence as well within religions that have been dominated by the masculine metaphor. Consider the Divine Presence experienced as the feminine Shekhinah and the Sabbath Queen in Jewish tradition. Another instance is the universal veneration among Muslims of the Virgin Mary and of Fatima, daughter of the Prophet of Islam. The principle names of Allah—Compassionate and Merciful, Rahman and Rahim—both derive from the Arabic root that signifies womb.

Indeed, everywhere we look in ancient or modern life, the nurturing, maturing, educating, and liberating power of the Divine Feminine can be seen in operation at the deepest levels of cultural wisdom. She operates directly through humanity, primarily through women but also through men; Neopagan, feminist, wise woman, traditional native, tantric, ecological, green, and creation-centered movements in contemporary society are reestablishing conscious communion with the Goddess on an increasingly wide scale.

From the most simple, basic point of view, for several years during infancy and early childhood, both female and male children relate in essentially the same mode and with the same intensity to the mother love at the core of their daily existence. The one we call father is at first simply mother number two, with bearded or abrasive face. Every longing is for mother. All sustenance is mother. Even the infant's landscape, before and after birth, is simply mother. For nine months, her heartbeat is our rhythm, our primal music. This is the original ground, prior to gender differentiation and sharp individuation, to which Goddess tradition gives us access, not as an infantile regression but as the fruitful soil of reconciliation, harmony, tenderness without boundary, unitive wisdom, and totality. That the great Indian poet of the Mother, Ramprasad, blossomed through a male body only shows that the ecstatic sensitivity, the all-embracing heart, the merciless honesty and diamond courage of Mother's most intimate companions are not fundamentally dependent on the biologically and culturally conditioned abstractions, *masculine* and *feminine*.

The basic cry of Ramprasad is *Ma! Ma! Ma!* What child is not crying out something like this wherever she or he may be on the planet or in planetary history? Is not Mother Reality always at the core of human experience, at the center of our spiritual hunger and thirst, and therefore at the heart of our integrity? Can we keep the Universal Mother as the central focus of our daily awareness, as the basis of a new global civilization?

Goddess tradition is much richer than any stereotypical notion of mother worship. Its practitioners are not interested in projecting a cosmic mother figure any more than they would project a cosmic father figure. The goal of spirituality is to realize truth, not to engage in projection and fantasy. Through Ramprasad's songs, the Goddess reveals herself as Woman Warrior, Teacher, Mother, and Consort. In different moods, she appears youthful, ancient, or ageless. These are actual dimensions of experience which can be entered by her devotees. She is divine creativity, evolutionary energy, timeless awareness, transcendent reality, and, in a special tantric sense, she is every woman. She constitutes the feminine principle within male and female persons and also manifests the gender-free feminine—self-luminous Mother Wisdom, nondual awareness and bliss.

Ramprasad experiences intimacy and union with the Goddess through all these diverse modes, through all her divine moods. Initiatory glimpses of his experience stream into the receptive reader. Through the living poems of Ramprasad, we can enter Mother's presence, commune with the entire spectrum of her manifestation, and gradually merge with her on every level of our being.

Ramprasad's Songs: Poetry or Initiation?

Mother Reality remains forever beyond words and concepts. She is basic indefinability yet reveals herself abundantly in every culture through poets and saints, who are windows for humanity. Seldom is one person strong enough to receive the double vocation of poet and saint. Such was Ramprasad, who lived his invisible life

4

of communion and union with the Goddess while surrounded by his extended family, working as a common clerk in eighteenth-century Bengal.

The explosion of awakened language which authentic poets experience after the pregnancy and contractions of creative birth can transform their individual being entirely, because the substance of humanity is infused with language. If the poetry is strong enough, the surrounding cultural body feels its impact and is transmuted, as dough is kneaded, rises through the potency of yeast, is baked, and becomes a new reality. For two hundred years, Bengal has been passionately singing the songs of Ramprasad and experiencing their power of transformation. The bread is ready.

The holy adventure of the saint, by contrast, is more a silent implosion than an explosion of language. Sanctity is secret inwardness. The poet longs to proclaim poetry, whereas the saint must conceal the incomprehensible fire of divine love. To reveal it to an admiring audience would be unthinkable. The poet carefully retains a critical literary taste and cultivates a unique personal sensibility. For sainthood, by contrast, the special personality must be constantly abandoned and eventually drowned in the ocean of love.

How can the vocations of saint and poet be combined? For the Divine Mother, the impossible is always becoming possible. The liberty of the poet and the liberation of the gnostic saint fuse in Ramprasad to create a fountain of metaphor and blessing. His spontaneous songs are both poetry and initiation. They are not simply songs about Mother Reality. They are Mother Reality. The sensitive reader can feel her direct touch.

Whoever loves the thrill of liberty, which is the authentic poetic experience, will appreciate these wildly metaphysical, allegorical, and yet intensely honest and personal poems. The voice of Ramprasad is surprisingly contemporary. Whoever has experienced the fragrance of divine love or glimpsed the secret path of mystic union will find deep springs of inspiration in the naked longing and ecstatic abandon of Ramprasad. Finally, whoever is drawn to the way of nondual awareness that transcends personality, religion, and culture will find sure guidance in the fearless wisdom of this poet. Mother Wisdom is essentially the way of nonduality. The Goddess is limitless, self-luminous space.

Not only do these songs tangibly present the sacrament of the Feminine Divine, they constitute an intimate journal of personal struggle, the evolutionary experience of a gifted mind and heart. In Ramprasad's complaints to the one he calls *my blissful Mother,* his arguments with her, and her powerful resolutions of his every doubt, we encounter the inner dynamic of contemplative life, which is not documented by religious textbooks or streamlined hagiographies. The bliss of beatific vision alternates with the anguish of limitation in a poetry of frankness, humor, and exultation.

Her Mysterious Appearance

Ramprasad's descriptions of the Goddess—whom he addresses as *Ma Kali, Ma Tara,* and simply as *Mother* or *Ma*—are not just rehearsals of traditional imagery but the profound elucidation of that imagery by the Wisdom Goddess, appearing to her poet and speaking through him. Ramprasad often assumes the persona of Mother's child, although the poetry reveals him as an extremely mature human being.

Kali appears through these songs as the beautiful black Warrior Goddess of unitive wisdom—wearing a garland of skulls, bearing weapons, dancing with fierce bliss on the breast of her supine consort, Shiva. This mode of appearing is strikingly different, for instance, from apparitions of the Virgin Mary; although in Eastern Orthodox tradition, the Virgin can appear as the victorious leader of triumphant hosts and, in the West, through figures such as Saint Joan of Arc.

Warrior Goddess Kali is not human imagination running wild

6

but an authentic self-revelation of Ultimate Reality, poured forth over many centuries in the tantric kingdom of Bengal and refocused through the refined perception of Ramprasad. Contemplating the awesome form of Goddess Kali, which always remains transparent to formless awareness, the human psyche is thoroughly shaken, purified, clarified, elevated, liberated, and illuminated. She is not a projection from our personal or collective psyche, as the modern world view would have us believe. She is the psyche in its wholeness, as she is the entire creation. And she is divine creativity which brings creation forth, moment by moment, as pure play or display. The way of Mother Wisdom, always marked by playfulness and surprise, is the gradual realization of her indivisible wholeness, which is our own essential nature, timeless awareness.

The mystery of Kali, impenetrable to conventional, dualistic thinking, is her blackness, her beautiful midnight blackness. The Goddess tradition, along with many other authentic spiritual transmissions during planetary history, fundamentally emphasizes divine inconceivability, the indefinability of Reality. The rich darkness within what Christian mystics call the Cloud of Unknowing is the radiant blackness of Mother's womb. Ramprasad is a consummate poet of this dazzling divine darkness:

> Why is Mother Kali so radiantly black?
> Because she is so powerful,
> that even mentioning her name destroys delusion.
> Because she is so beautiful,
> Lord Shiva, Conqueror of Death,
> lies blissfully vanquished
>   beneath her red-soled feet.
> There are subtle hues of blackness,
> but her bright complexion
>   is the mystery that is utterly black,
> overwhelmingly black, wonderfully black.
> When she awakens in the lotus shrine
>   within the heart's secret cave,

her blackness becomes the mystic illumination
that causes the twelve-petal blossom there
to glow more intensely than golden embers.
Whoever gazes upon this radiant blackness
falls eternally in love.

This black light expresses the highest teaching of the Goddess. It is the radiance beyond whatever we know as light, yet at the same time it constitutes all physical, intellectual, and spiritual light. The full range of our experience is ignited by a small spark from this Mother Radiance, manifesting through our precious human form. As Ramprasad sings concerning her reality, so radically unapproachable by the intellect and yet so intimate with our being: "Who in the world can know what Mother Kali really is? She is beyond the reach of every scripture, every system of philosophy. She plays as the radiant blackness of divine mystery through the lotus wilderness of the sacred human body."

The Warrior Goddess strikes terror into minds and hearts only if they cling to intellectual or emotional limits. Her garland of skulls attests to freedom from every conventional or existential limit, including the apparently ultimate limits of birth and death. This terrible garland is the supreme adornment of liberating insight and is thus charming and beautiful to mature lovers of the Goddess—never fearsome, depressing, ghastly. The awesome vision of Kali exposes all intellectual and emotional evasions. It cuts through the thick walls constructed by conventional religion and breaks open other cultural structures which have become vehicles for the separative, dominating ego.

The doctrines of reincarnation, heaven, hell, complete extinction after death, liberation from the wheel of time, and even mystic union are all cut away with marvelous nonchalance by her sword of nondual wisdom. Ramprasad sings:

Everyone is babbling about what happens after death.

This intoxicated poet who belongs to Goddess Kali
knows all opinions to be void of substance.
This mirror mind and rainbow body
are her marvelous play
through the transparent medium of her elements.
After death, her dancing elements flow on,
and simply Mother remains.
The singer of this liberating song
laughs loud and long:
"We will be in the end
what we were in the beginning,
clear bubbles forming and dissolving
in the stream of timeless Mother Wisdom."

Liberation or Illumination?

The very nature of the playful Wisdom Goddess is to transcend philosophy and theology. She is invisible to the systematic gaze. Yet through Ramprasad's poems, written in a heightened, revelatory tongue, certain basic attitudes concerning the structure and value of the temporal world are hinted. The poems present what one could term a theology of the immanence and transcendence of Mother Reality.

Ramprasad longs to be liberated from the whirlwind of time, to reach calm harbor from the stormy ocean of generation and destruction. This liberation is most clearly likened to waking from dream. It is the brilliant dawning of her wisdom and her love that dissolve the pervasive obscurity and ambiguity of human existence, its perceptual, emotional, and conceptual egocentricity. The poet seeks from Mother this full awakening, this freedom from self, not only for himself but for all humanity and indeed for all conscious creatures.

Ramprasad has achieved the spiritual level of intense and continuous longing to be liberated by the Goddess into the Goddess. This is the underlying theme of his songs, which are not formal philosophy but direct, existential encounters with Mother Reality. This longing is not a dualistic reaching toward the Goddess but a play unfolding within the Goddess, a drama full of anguish and delight.

Ramprasad can confirm—from personal experience, not merely from scriptural study—the traditional Indian teaching that relative existence intoxicates, ensnares, and dissipates human consciousness by forcing it into the mold of egocentricity. Yet the poet's intimate experience of his blissful Mother adds a new dimension to this traditional ascetic and gnostic view of the world as a subtle trap. Mother Wisdom is tantric, which means that she reveals relative existence as her divine theater—in Ramprasad's words, "a country fair for those mad with love," or elsewhere, "the country fair of Mother's sheer delight." This surprising knowledge transforms Ramprasad into a *paramahamsa*, a completely unconventional sage, comfortable both within and beyond the borders of culture and religion: "Goddess Kali, you are the brilliant magician and I am your sleight-of hand. I dance as Mother dances through me. Mysterious Kali, you manifest as the virtuous practice of religion and as wild, rebellious action. This is your secret, your universal play." The goal of union with the Goddess is not liberation from the phenomenal world but total illumination, which embraces relative and absolute equally. Throughout Ramprasad's songs, this ideal of complete enlightenment is unveiled. There can be no division, no truncation.

The radical freedom of the Goddess does not tempt the poet-saint to lead the chaotic life of a libertine. He continues to hold his family responsibility and to perform his traditional worship, regarding both as Mother Reality fully manifest. This universe no longer appears as obsessive personal and cultural fantasy but as the free, limitless, illuminating dream of Mother. Experience is no longer meaningless suffering and bondage but mysterious dance, refreshment, and rest. It is no longer destructive, egocentric intoxication but the truly blissful inebriation of the Goddess. Life is now her experience, her play, even her brilliant illusion, rather than our project, our suffering, our delusion.

With almost every song, if not with every breath, the poet-saint moves back and forth between two vastly different perspectives, the human and the divine, the relative and the absolute, ultimately fusing them, without denying either side and without confusing them. This nondual vision is the measure of Ramprasad's deep spiritual maturity. He is neither utopian nor romantic but filled with ecstatic realism: "I will continue to accept the play of daily life as your most precious teaching, never ceasing to sing *Kali, Kali, Kali.*"

As he sings, Ramprasad is immersed in ecstasy, not philosophy. Crying *Ma! Ma! Ma!,* he approaches Reality with intense love and complete trust. He relies upon his Divine Mother alone to resolve the human dilemma. Our chronic disease is essentially bondage to separate individuality and substantiality as we habitually and even obsessively perceive them. This situation is diagnosed by Ramprasad as a degenerative form of insanity, a fatal inflation of the possessive, domineering ego which can be relieved only through encountering Mother Kali. The poet always identifies himself fully with this human condition, confessing: "The fruits of mundane existence drive me insane, causing me to claim the universe as mine alone, *my loved ones, my sense organs, mine, all mine!*"

Ramprasad describes the personal and collective madness of ego-centricity as a process of projection and reflection. True delight is not to be obtained by any complex strategy, whether worldly or religious, but simply by abiding as original awareness, prior to and beyond the process of projecting and reflecting: "This projected universe is only the faint reflection of Reality. By attempting to grasp reflected images, we cheat ourselves of true experience. Turn instead to the original, and discover the limitless treasure of delight."

In the realm of reflection, we encounter the inevitable evolution of countless physical and mental conditions, but the realmless realm of original awareness remains always simple and free, never conditioned or bound by the tension of subject and object. The phenomenal world, however, is none other than Mother's own infinite awareness. There is no duality.

> *This realm of reflection we encounter*
> *consists of mind, earth, wind, water,*
> *arranging and rearranging with increasing complexity.*
> *The principle of subtle energy*
> *evolves naturally into tangibility,*
> *blossoming as living worlds beyond number.*
> *A single sun reflects in countless water-bearing vessels.*
> *As these earthenware worlds are broken, one by one,*
> *the sunlight of primal awareness remains the same.*

The songs of Ramprasad are not intellectual or poetic descriptions but an open door to the direct experience of timeless awareness, which is not a mere empty expanse but dynamic, tender, playful, and, above all, blissful. Pure awareness is the Goddess: "The world of nature and culture is an intricate magical display. You have not yet encountered the brilliant Magician. She resides within each breath, each thought, each movement, each perception."

All Forms Embraced in Oneness

The universe in all its living detail appears vividly within the oneness or wholeness of blissful Mother Reality. Goddess Wisdom reveals all events, patterns, and meanings, including entire cultures and religions that cross cultural borders, as transparent to her, embraced within her: "All forms appear and disappear only within the formless mystery of Mother. O Goddess, nothing exists except your bliss, your illumination, your play, and your names." This openness to her mystery leads to the supreme insight: "This is the dawning of enlightenment, the awakening to nonduality. Her form and every form are now blending into one radiant blackness. O mind, despise no being, reject no path. See all in her and her as all."

At this peak of revelatory experience, Mother alone is perceived, in and through every manifestation, including the perceiver. Ramprasad meets Goddess energy through the religious diversity around him in Bengal, seeing all approaches harmonized by the single cry *Ma! Ma! Ma!*, the mystic Motherhood beyond all divine names and esoteric teachings.

> *Sometimes you appear as the peaceful helpmate*
> *   seated beside Shiva in quiet harmony.*
> *Sometimes you manifest as the radiant cosmos*
> *   and its countless living beings.*
> *Sometimes you play as the incomparable Radha,*
> *courageous lover of Lord Krishna.*
> *Other times you manifest as Mother Kundalini,*
> *the evolutionary potency*
> *   coiled at the root of the subtle body.*
> *But this mad poet refuses to pay heed*
> *   to any theology, any philosophy.*
> *I can only weep:*
> Ma, Ma, Ma!
> *This is your sweetest name,*
> *transcending all descriptions.*

Once awake within Mother Reality, there is no more fear of dying, and therefore the therapeutic remembrance of death is no longer necessary: "Simply utter *Kali, Kali, Kali.* The agony of death will vanish instantly." Cries Ramprasad: "Listen to me, Death, so your insane pride will at last be humbled. You can take away only this form. I have already begun my deathless journey, chanting *Ma Kali, Ma Kali.*" Elsewhere he states his relation to death more bluntly: "From the Mother of the Universe, whose divine authority is absolute, I have received the clear order that Death must die." This is the radical tantric way of transmutation, or total illumination.

There is no opposing force at this level of realization, not even a shadow of ignorance: "I can now evoke your sparkling energy at the very root of this body. You are no longer able to conceal yourself or appear distant from me. My very breath and being bond with your potent mystery. I know and I know that I know. No one can remove this realization. Not even you." Or elsewhere, simply: "Who can keep a blazing fire tied in a cotton cloth?"

Total and ceaseless intimacy with his blissful Mother is what distinguishes Ramprasad's life from the conventional function of religious ritual, which is the seeking of solace, just as it distinguishes his songs from any system of philosophy or theology, which is the seeking of certainty. The Godhead, who is the sublime object of theology, remains far below Ramprasad's Divine Mother. Drunkenly, Ramprasad sings: "Who is she? At her uncrossable threshold of mystery the Creator and Preserver of the universe stands in awe and supplication." This is not theology but simply the rapturous cry with which Ramprasad, in the mood of spiritual warrior, confronts humanity: "You know almost nothing concerning Mother's grandeur. She is the infinite dream power of reality. She is the dynamic play of pure consciousness." We find ourselves suddenly embraced by her open space, far beyond the realm of religion.

Awakening into Pure Love

We have previously considered the transcendent insight of Ramprasad—his *gnosis,* or liberating knowledge. This blissful knowing prepares the way for the ultimate realization, which can only occur through love. As Ramprasad expresses this subtle relationship: "The priceless pearl of love is manifest only at the uttermost depth of Mother's wisdom ocean." The poet's extraordinary love is not emotional or even devotional, being free from any structure of subject and object. As such, it achieves the infinite intensity of nonduality.

A key to understanding this most inclusive experience is the recognition that pure love is not a state of attainment which belongs to any particular person, nor is it a doctrine which could be taught by any religious teacher. It is the life of enlightened play, the very life of the Goddess: "She alone is the one who meditates through aspirants who belong to every spiritual way." The entire human dilemma in all its seriousness is dissolved by pure love, leaving the full range of our personal experience and responsibility still in play. As Ramprasad writes: "Mother, your dream-play universe is sheer delight. Souls caught in the seriousness of your drama are constantly running, looking for release. But souls who know their own boundless nature are free and happy under every condition."

To recognize the impossibility of approaching Mother Reality through philosophy, theology, or contemplative exercise does not leave us in a state of frustration but opens the gate of fulfillment: "This very universe becomes a radiant garden of bliss for those who repeat her name with every heartbeat, every breath." But philosophers, priests, and yogis who cling to their own particular habitual standards and practices cannot enter this wonderful garden of nonduality, although the Goddess throws its seven gates wide open: "Mother's mystery eludes every earnest practitioner or philosopher who assumes negative or positive energy to be substantial or real."

The Wisdom Goddess does not excuse the self-imposed limitations of various worshipers and thinkers: "You know the single truth, O mind, with clarity and certainty. Your very nature is this truth. Why do you imagine constantly that you are ignorant?" Her warning is directed as well to the arguments between denominations or world religions. Through Ramprasad, the Goddess pointedly asks: "Why are you unable to perceive the embracing unity behind every manifestation of Divinity? Still confused by multiplicity, your eloquent prayers remain hypocrisy. With eyes wide open and functioning, you remain totally blind." Expressing universal human aspiration, the poet-saint cries with burning sincerity: "Even your devoted ones, Gautama, Moses, Krishna, Jesus, Nanak, and Muhammad, are lost in the rapture of pure love. When will I be granted companionship with your intense lovers?"

Without attempting to systematize Mother Wisdom, we can follow these songs of Ramprasad into the very heart of her reality: "This is the dawning of enlightenment, the awakening to nonduality. Her form and every form are now blending into one radiant blackness." The enlightenment experience is fundamentally the bliss that flows into human consciousness from the great bliss of the Goddess: "The most exalted experience of bliss in any realm of being is directly knowing the universal Mother, the supremely blissful one." Not just an ultimate attainment for awakened sages, this taste of divine bliss, in varying degrees of intensity, is available for all humanity, for all conscious beings. It is the essence of awareness. There is no elitism along the way of the Mother. Calling out compassionately to his sisters and brothers throughout time, Ramprasad queries: "What use is this marvelous human body if it does not dance in holy ecstasy? Blind the eyes that do not perceive every creature as a blissful expression of the Cosmic Mother." This total Mother-orientation is as essential for a fruitful personal life as it is for a harmonious global civilization.

What is the state of one who awakens into the pure love called Mother Reality? The realized poet describes this most exalted experience rather casually: "Who cares for traveling to every sacred planetary place? I simply long to breathe with each breath, as though it were my last, *Ma Kali, Ma Kali, Ma Kali.*" This blissful inclination to cease traveling in search of absolute truth, either outwardly or inwardly, arises spontaneously in the awakened mind: "O mind, awaken to your innate purity and be perfectly at rest. You must not travel anywhere, even the slightest distance. You will receive the treasure of illumination at the very heart and ground of your being." Enlightenment must be experienced here in the global village, here in the extended family, here in the tribulation and delight of being fully human: "You will receive Mother's breath of wisdom while sitting at home in quiet contemplation, disciplined by the responsibility of daily life."

Ramprasad's Path of Practice

By following certain rich veins in these esoteric hymns, we can glimpse the radical way of contemplation which Ramprasad inherited from the tantric culture of Bengal and which the Goddess revealed directly to him during a lifetime of intimate communion with her.

The spiritual path is essentially a form of awakening. At the initial stages of practice, the qualified teacher never ceases to remind the student of basic human ignorance, the tendency to remain asleep with eyes still open, a habit which persists long after the efforts of meditation have begun. Sings Ramprasad: "O my dreaming mind, awaken now and remain awake forever! Sleeping with eyes open as you walk through the world is the strange sleep of delusion."

There is fundamentally but one teacher, one spiritual guide: the innately enlightened awareness that is primordial light, shining forth as spontaneous manifestations of pure love. This universal teaching power, the essence of awareness, is experienced by Ramprasad as his tender, playful, mysterious Mother Kali. She is encountered in countless contrasting modes by awakened saints and sages from other traditions. This teaching power, this Mother Wisdom, is the single reservoir of deep coherence and liberating ecstasy drawn from by every culture and by every person. This Mother Reality inaugurates all the noble religious traditions and continues to revitalize them over centuries and millennia. Mother Reality appears through divine forms as formless radiance and as fully awakened human beings who skillfully demonstrate the spiritual way to all.

The enlightened human friend and guide, who is usually an essential factor in the process of realization, simply points with her or his own inclusive awareness to the Divine Teacher and then graciously steps aside. Ramprasad evidently enjoyed the sweet companionship of an enlightened human teacher as well as mystical encounters with celestial forms of the Divine Mother. This makes the poet-saint an inheritor of the horizontal historical lineage as well as a recipient of the vertical lightning flash of Mother's grace. As he confirms: "My beloved human guide, ocean of mercy, selfless friend of all who seek refuge, showed me the bright wisdom feet of the Goddess, dancing and shining in my heart. Through the holy companionship of my mentor, the Mother of the Universe has come to dwell in my home."

As intimacy with the Goddess develops, she becomes the primary guide and eventually the sole Beloved, appearing everywhere and speaking through all creatures. Religious rites and yogic disciplines become outmoded: "Why worship with such profusion of jewels and lamps? Unveil the self-radiant diamond of your essence, O mind, and allow it alone to illuminate the heart's secret shrine day and night." As her ecstatic child sings: "Why should one who experiences all as Mother perform finite worship? Who is there to meditate on whom?"

There is, however, an appropriate inward attitude at this level of development. Ramprasad presents the Wisdom Mother's own instructions for liberated contemplation: "Consider the simple act of lying down to sleep as devoted offering of your whole body and mind to her. Allow your dreams to become radiant meditations on the Cosmic Mother. As you wander through countryside or city, feel that you are moving through *Kali, Kali, Kali.* All sounds you hear are her natural mantras, arising spontaneously as the whole universe worships her." This ultimate contemplative mood is beyond formal meditation: "With this pure mind, practice the meditation beyond all meditation. You will attain final success in spiritual life, the enlightenment of the whole being, including all its passionate intensity." More openly, Ramprasad reveals: "Recognize your very existence, no matter how you live, as her changeless diamond nature."

This practice of nondualistic devotion, which frees awareness from the convention of subject and object, can be embraced only by those who offer to the Goddess every desire, whether worldly or religious. As the Divine Mother encourages humanity through the voice of

Ramprasad: "O longing mind, focus all your longing on Mother Kali. You will receive pure love and liberating knowledge, tangibly as fruits placed on the palm of the hand." This approach is based in the tantric principle that transforms all experience, however unrefined, into the path of ecstatic love and freedom. As Ramprasad sings: "I will tame the primal obsessions of greed, anger, pride, hatred, and use them as powerful bullocks to plow the field of consciousness." This path is already immersed in the goal.

In this tantric way of immediate fruition, in which the goal itself is taken as the path, lovers of the Goddess achieve spontaneously and harmoniously, free from subtle bonds of spiritual pride, the intensity and freedom which is the aim of stern ascetic discipline: "Those who have made Kali's feet of infinite delight the only goal and meaning of their life spontaneously forget every craving for egocentric power and pleasure." Thus the entire being, including every organ of the body, becomes open toward the Goddess and attuned sensitively to her: "Can the Mother of the Universe be embraced unless every organ of action and perception becomes oriented toward her? Can the thorny scrub tree bear sweet fruit?" Awakening as Mother Reality must become our central, animating motivation—our present moment, our indescribable joy. The principle of Mother's tantric way is to avoid any truncation of human reality, any separation between human and divine, between relative and absolute. This is the way of nonduality.

Seven Lotus Centers and Kundalini

How can this apparently simple requirement of holding Mother's presence at the center of awareness actually be fulfilled, breath by breath? The Goddess responds with the esoteric tradition of kundalini, the evolutionary energy of primal awareness which rises through six lotus centers, or *chakras,* within the subtle dimension of the nervous system, and pours into the seventh *chakra,* the thousand-petal lotus of reality. Kundalini is not physiological, although it affects the physiology. Kundalini is Mother in all her fullness.

Three principle channels containing her conscious energy intersect at six nodes, creating six spirals of consciousness, each one clearer and more intense. This pattern of energy channels and centers constitutes the esoteric dimension of the human body. The thousand-petal lotus at the crown is nondual awareness—the ultimate reality of the Mother, who remains open space even while she manifests as heavenly, subtle, and earthly realms that express her dynamic plenitude.

The awakening person ascends in consciousness through these six lotus centers. They are the evolutionary body of humanity, which is correlated with the biological body but not confined to it. As each lotus blossoms, higher, more radiant, more comprehensive dimensions of experience open. The illumination generated by the awakening of the higher centers in the subtle body enhances the experiential realms of the lower centers as well, purifying personal and collective experience from the dross of egocentricity.

Thus the voyager of the Mother is enabled to perceive the entire subtle body of humanity, the full spectrum of human awareness, as a single sacred landscape, at once communal and personal. Separative ego is not necessary for genuine relationship or authentic personhood; in fact, egocentricity obscures these treasures of full humanity. Therefore, Ramprasad sings: "O Mother of the Universe, please sever with your brilliant sword of wisdom the bonds of egocentric thought and action, and allow my soul's light to rise through the crown of my head, the gateway to total illumination." Entering the thousand-petal Mother Reality at the crown of the subtle body, lovers of the Goddess are fully liberated and enlightened while still living on earth.

Ramprasad reports on this wonderful landscape of Mother's play, which we call humanity, not as esoteric doctrine but from direct personal experience: "The twelve-petal lotus that floats in my chest is surrounded by her fierce flames. I contemplate with awe the thousand-petal lotus at my crown where the golden honey of mystic union is flowing eternally. O Mother Kundalini, my entire being is swept upward continuously by your current of wisdom energy." Ramprasad describes Mother Kundalini as "the great swan ever swimming through the lotus jungle of the subtle body."

However, this revolutionary poet of the Mother is not a conventional yogi. Rather than following a long course of exploration through these various levels of awareness, the radical poet-saint of Bengal ecstatically proclaims: "I now offer her the seven subtle lotus centers of the pristine spiritual body, and the booming drum of realization at once announces the conquest of mortality." With characteristic humility and abandon, Ramprasad discards the entire project of kundalini yoga, which contains its own potential for spiritual pride, and requests the Goddess simply to manifest in him as she wishes, through the medium of his mind and heart, purified and well-tuned by her.

> *O Kali of Mystery!*
> *I yearn to hold your luminous power*
>   *in the subtle nerve channels near the spine*
> *long enough to know you more intensely.*
> *Yet your brilliant Goddess energy*
>   *dances with freedom and wild abandon.*
> *How can I possibly contain you, even for an instant?*
> *May you come to rest gently*
>   *upon the spacious lotus of my heart,*
> *playing with pure awareness*
>   *the many-stringed instrument of my mind.*

Meditating on Her Presence

All prayers of sacred traditions, even the basic cultural process of verbal expression itself, are perceived by the penetrating insight of Ramprasad to be spontaneous mantras that evoke Mother Reality. The mystic poet sings: "The Goddess, who is unitive wisdom, constitutes the letters of every alphabet. Every word secretly bears the power of her name." However, this sense of her pervasive presence must be achieved, not merely imagined.

Genuine release from the mundane categories of egocentric experience comes only to those who are willing to part with their mundane head: "If you wish to be liberated from oppression, abandon whatever limits you cling to and meditate on the limitless one who wears limitation as a garland of heads, freshly severed by her sword of nondual wisdom." It is interesting to note that in the traditional iconography of Kali, her garland always consists of freshly severed male heads, smiling, free at last from their archetypal masculine role of domination. Elsewhere the poet asks, with his droll humor: "If the head is gone, can the headache remain?" Meditating on her presence, one loses one's head beneath her merciful sword, that is, one undergoes a fundamental revolution of consciousness. The devotee of the Goddess experiences a great, life-giving storm: "This lover of Ma Kali gazes intently, tears pouring down like monsoon rain." No conventional, habitual separateness can remain: "Dedicate your life to her indivisible presence. Transform your being into a full expression of her being." There can be no fundamental duality between worshiped and worshiper along the tantric way of the Mother.

Radical simplicity is the core of Mother Wisdom, beyond all forms of contemplative practice, beyond all hierarchy. This wisdom is the spontaneous shining forth of indivisible awareness. Ramprasad sings: "Lovers who travel her way beyond meditation receive all-embracing Mother Wisdom, empowering the mind to discard completely every egocentric attraction or repulsion by focusing awareness solely on its own innate purity, its natural self-luminosity."

The intrinsic nature of our awareness, when it becomes purified from extraneous conventions, is love. Ultimately, the only spiritual practice or way of life Ramprasad recommends is love. He sings, with tears of nondual devotion flowing down his cheeks, dampening his upper garment: "Make me totally drunk with the wine of your all-embracing love. Immerse me irretrievably in the stormy ocean of your love. Who can fathom your mystery, your eternal play of love with love?"

The madness of this love is true sanity, total humanity. It is the completeness of the passionate person who has not been truncated by ascetic dualism or made abstract by stubborn adherence to religious or philosophical doctrine. Ramprasad calls those who would separate the Divine Mother from her radiant creation mad, in the negative sense: "O misguided mind, are you mad? How can you worship the Mother of the Universe by sitting in a dark room, legs crossed, eyes closed, breath in suspension? She is the play of boundless affection. No one can realize her embracing reality who is not consumed by the fire of love." And elsewhere: "Can you see? The realms of being that you separate habitually, calling them heaven and earth, divinity and humanity, are simply forms of one universal Mother." Ramprasad asks us to share this sublime vision. Can we, too, perceive that human beings are exquisite forms of the Mother?

Warrior Goddess

The bearer of the sword of unitive wisdom is a warrior Goddess of great bliss. She is not the passive, merely nurturing Mother from the library of cultural and religious stereotypes. Neither is Kali the dark and destructive Mother she has been misunderstood to be from a literal reading of her iconography by Western scholars, nor is she the fearsome figure depicted by some superstitious Indian village piety.

Mother Kali's field of battle is the complex network of mental and physical suffering. Her enemy is the aggressive and even demonic force of self-inflation. Her weapon is enlightened energy. Ramprasad cries out: "The singer of this mystic hymn is overwhelmed by the sudden vision of Kali as supreme Warrior of Wisdom, roaming the battleground of universal suffering, dissolving the demons of egocentricity with her terrible cry of power." She neither creates nor destroys; she simply reveals and illumines. Her splendid warfare is sheer compassion, entirely transcending any ordinary notion of conflict. The very concept of war, which springs from the delusive sense of separation, is one of the dangerous demonic forces that she vanquishes as it arises again and again through the chronic egocentricity of individuals and societies.

Kali the Warrior Woman, in her unique mode of transcendent meaning, is indeed a goddess streaming with blood. Bloodless warfare would be like bloodless life, an empty abstraction, whereas the Mother of the Universe is the existential primacy at the opposite pole from abstraction. Sings the powerful poet of the Mother: "All blood ever shed in sacrifice or conflict streams down her brilliant black limbs like crimson blossoms floating on dark waters."

What is this warrior attitude of Goddess Wisdom, totally free from the cruelty and destructiveness of mundane war-making? Ramprasad hints at the sublime attitude of Kali, whose very glance is a consuming fire: "She laughs aloud, regarding relative existence as one vast cremation ground." She does not engage in limited warfare but destroys with her bliss the very principle of oppositional duality on every level, revealing instead her enchanting beauty. Through the door of Mother's beauty, one enters the dazzling darkness beyond light which various sacred traditions call Enlightenment.

Chariots and drivers, horses and horsemen,
arrows and archers, she devours whole.
Elephants of war stampede and are lost in her as moths
*   consumed by flame.*
The incomparable light of Kali's beauty
*   pervades the universe,*
as she swallows into her dazzling darkness
*   the ferocious array of demonic passions.*
She has destroyed the narrow hopes
*   of every limited self in creation*
by consuming the objective and subjective worlds
*   in ecstatic conflagration.*

24

All beings must now renounce
conventional projects and projections.
None will survive the fury of her illumination.

In order to remove divisions and boundaries, our emerging global civilization must receive and assimilate this teaching of the Warrior Goddess, perhaps strange to the modern ear, yet ever near to the human heart.

Her Divine Consort

We must remember Goddess Kali's voluntary relationship with her consort, Lord Shiva. The Goddess is inwardly independent of her counterpart in male form, for she has no need of the masculine principle to complete her, much less to assist or protect her. She embraces all possibilities within her as she strides alone across the universal field of battle or dances in the ecstasy of nonduality. Out of her very plenitude, she chooses blissful union with Shiva, a union in which she is the dominant partner, dancing fiercely or standing perfectly still upon his vast breast, which is the peaceful expanse of the absolute.

Through Ramprasad, the Wisdom Goddess is calling humanity to ecstatic freedom from all traces of conventional, habitual thought and perception. She is the sublime outer feminine as all women and the inner feminine within women and men. But primarily she is the secret, gender-free feminine, the open space of unitive wisdom which Ramprasad calls "the radiant blackness of her womb." Not only does the touch of her feet inebriate Shiva and her other intimate worshipers, both women and men, but these flashing feet of mystery dissolve the laws of nature, freeing our entire universe from its conventionally perceived tendency toward rigidity or inertia. Our routine constructions of what is real, be they perceptual, scientific, rational, mythological, or religious, are consumed by the blazing fire of Kali, leaving us in the state of Shiva, absorbed in limitless Mother Reality. Shiva, perfect knower and pure knowledge, not only contemplates the Goddess but is dissolved into her. This blessed awakening into the Goddess that discovers her as the essence of awareness, as our own most intimate essence, occurs eventually to every knower of truth, to every Shiva. After this supreme awakening, only Kali remains.

"If you wish to be liberated from oppression," sings Ramprasad, speaking about oppression by conventional thinking, be it cultural or metaphysical, "abandon whatever limits you cling to." As the poet-saint reveals, at the highest level of teaching: "Lord Shiva, the sublime Knower of Reality, fearless one on whom seekers of transcendent truth rely, casts away his divine form at her feet of bliss. With her indescribable love, she has now destroyed the very Destroyer of Death." Nothing can resist the Warrior Goddess. She has now even consumed Shiva, the essence of divinity.

Portrait of Ramprasad

What did Ramprasad look like, seated in the small, busy courtyard of his home? "They are in constant contact only with the root and essence of reality. What do they care for the opinion of the world? These lovers, eyes half-closed with inward gaze, are drinking night and day the sweet and powerful nectar, Mother! Mother! Mother!" What did the poet look like as he walked to the river Ganges for his daily bath? "My essence has already plunged into your essence. I continue to appear simply as an empty wooden frame in human form, moved about and held together by Mother's inscrutable power."

Ramprasad's disappearance into the Divine Mother is so profound that only she can evaluate it: "You alone can discern who you are and who I am. Is there any distinction?" To be in the direct presence of such union, whether the saint sits indrawn in ecstasy or moves through the world like an empty wooden frame, can be unsettling or uplifting, depending upon our own level of receptivity and the intensity of our attachment to the convention of separate individuality. Ramprasad is simply the embodiment of Goddess Kali. There is no one else.

The poet-saint's every action, his very mind and being, are tantric songs, not simply those which have been recorded with ink on paper. Cries this supreme mystic: "My life has become her own contemplation." The Divine Mother is not the slightest distance, either physical or spiritual, from her illumined devotee, who is the ultimately precocious child, the adept of pure love. He sings: "How can I say you are distant from me?" Elsewhere he proclaims most boldly: "She has become my very body! Even this is only a hint, O mind. There is nothing apart from her reality."

We can picture Ramprasad moving through the streets of the bazaar, reeling with bliss, being greeted heartily by local drunkards: "Today my whole being is so sweetly reeling with Mother's own drunken love that even those soaked in ordinary wine consider me one of them!" Ramprasad strolls through the marketplace, singing madly: "O sisters and brothers, friends of truth, please cherish no hope for this poet, who is lost completely to the world of individuality."

As we finally lose sight of the poet, blending among the populace, disappearing into the green landscape of Bengal, his songs remain in the depth of our awareness as a vibrant transmission. We can now hear his voice as our own, directly confronting our own mind: "Mother exists also as each life form, each event. Open your foolish eyes and perceive the Goddess everywhere. Even the deepest darkness of this world is simply her light." With Ramprasad's own fervor, we sing: "This poet lover pleads with everyone: 'Please pass your lifetime repeating *Ma! Ma! Ma!* Entrust your breath and being to the Mother!'"

Who is Mother? Where is Mother? The Goddess speaks strongly through Ramprasad, who is our own precious human voice: "Now lift the curtain of relative existence and gaze into your own original face!"

Tantric Hymns of Enlightenment

Please be gracious to the singer of this song!

O Mother of the Universe! Flowing power of the Absolute!
Purifier of all minds and hearts!
You who confer your own bliss
    as the sublime fruit of the spiritual quest!
O ecstatic consort of the Absolute!
You who enchant the Absolute!
Grant me the fragrant shade of your lotus feet
    on this most auspicious day!

Ma! Ma! Ma!
You who liberate every conscious being!
Please shower your grace, your total illumination!
I am a simple person
    without sublime gifts of character.
I lack intensity in my life of prayer.
My blissful Mother, only you can awaken me
    from this dream of change,
this magic theater of temporality.

Most compassionate Ma Tara!
You who bear all beings tenderly to truth!
Your feet of wisdom are the only vessel that can sail
    across this terrible sea of birth and death.
Mysterious Ma Kali!
Consort and Power of Absolute Reality!
You who are one with Reality!
Please be present! Please absorb me!
Please be gracious to the singer of this song!

31

Satisfy every level of our hunger!

O Mother of the Universe!
You who provide basic sustenance
    and subtle nourishment for all creatures!
Please feed us, Holy Mother!
Satisfy every level of our hunger!

I know the mother always feeds her hungry child,
regardless of its foolishness or carelessness.
Goddess Kali, grant the child who sings this song
    your supreme blessing of total illumination.
Today is the most auspicious day!
Please, Mother, do not delay!

Goddess Tara, my pangs of hunger for reality
    are becoming unbearable.
Mother! Mother! Mother!
You are the longing and the longed for!
You cannot refuse your child's earnest prayer!

Entrust your breath and being to the Mother!

O tongue, form with every breath
the powerful name of transformation,
Ma Kali, Ma Kali.
The heart where Goddess Kali is awake
feels no need to reason or speculate.

Simply to satisfy our longing, we consecrate
external images for worship of the Goddess.
She abides deep in our inward being
as open space, as dancing flame.

O singer of Mother's mystic hymns,
bring your scattered speech together
and taste the nectar of her name.
Silently or aloud,
chant her glorious name at every step,
with every perception, every intention,
drinking the inebriating sweetness,
Kali, Kali, Kali.
You are a simpleminded poet
suited to this simple way.

Her living name is a fountain of delight,
streaming with the ambrosia of timeless awareness.
Chant this name ten thousand times each day,
counting with your fingers.
Is this too difficult a task,
O foolish one who sings her songs?

Listen with inward ear to the music
of her wisdom, teaching all creation.
With inward eye visualize her brilliant name,
flowing across your heart in letters of molten gold.

Free from shame or hesitation,
this poet lover pleads with everyone:
"Please pass your lifetime repeating *Ma! Ma! Ma!*
Entrust your breath and being to the Mother!"

This poet can only cry in ecstasy

O Wisdom Goddess!
Your essence alone is present
    within every life, every event.
Your living power flows freely as this universe.
You are expressed fully, even by the smallest movement.
Wherever I go and wherever I look,
I perceive only you, my blissful Mother,
radiating as pure cosmic play.
Earth, water, fire, air, space, and consciousness
    are simply your projected forms.
There is nothing else.

Ma! Ma! Ma!
Your lucid dream of light
    is the theater of birth and death,
the expanse of boundless transparency.

This poet can only cry in ecstasy:
"Green mountains, fragrant blossoms,
countless lives on land and beneath the sea,
animate beings and inanimate objects
    are composed of Mother's reality,
and spontaneously express her will."

Though my mind wanders everywhere, I am not to blame

Though my mind wanders everywhere,
I am not to blame.
Goddess Kali, you are the brilliant magician
    and I am your sleight-of-hand.
I dance as Mother dances through me.

Mysterious Kali, you manifest
    as the virtuous practice of religion
and as wild, rebellious action.
This is your secret, your universal play.

You alone are fertile earth and flowing waters,
and you are the conscious energy behind the universe.
You are burning love experienced by lovers
    and calm illumination in the hearts of sages.
This oneness is revealed by Shiva,
your intimate consort, O Wisdom Mother,
who is plunged into luminous rapture
    by the touch of your dancing feet.

Mother alone manifests light and darkness,
delight and despair,
as esoteric scriptures of the Goddess make clear.
Inebriated by her mystery,
this poet lover weeps and sings:
"The thread of my life is spun
    on the cosmic spinning wheel
of action and reaction.
Mad with the bliss of oneness,
Ma Kali and her consort, Absolute Reality,
weave innumerable lives, magic threads on a single loom,
causing them to enact spontaneously
    the wonderful dream-play of the universe."

The total madness of her love

Mother dwells at the center of my being,
forever delightfully at play.
Whatever conditions of consciousness may arise,
I hear through them the music of her life-giving names,
    Om Tara, Om Kali.

Closing my eyes, I perceive the radiant Black Mother
    as indivisible, naked awareness,
dancing fiercely or gently on my heart lotus.
She wears a garland of snow-white skulls,
bright emblem of freedom from birth and death.
Gazing upon her resplendent nakedness,
all concepts and conventions vanish.

Those who judge by mundane standards call me mad.
Timid and limited persons can think what they wish.
My only longing is to express
    the total madness of her love.

This poet child of the Wisdom Goddess
    cries out with abandon:
"The Queen of the Universe
    resides within the flower of my secret heart.
Mother! Mother! Mother!
I seek refuge at your beautiful feet,
delicate and fragrant as the dark blue lotus.
As my body dissolves into earth
    and my mind into space,
may I dissolve into you."

Every conflict in my life has been resolved

The name of Kali is divinely sweet to taste.
Chant *Om Kali Ma* with every breath,
drinking the nectar of her unitive wisdom.
Shame on you, my foolish tongue,
still craving the ordinary tastes
     of an ordinary world.

All forms appear and disappear
     within the formless mystery of Mother.
O Goddess, nothing exists except your bliss,
your illumination, your play, and your names.
The all-purifying river, Mother Ganga,
flows through every heart where Kali is awake.
Even Absolute Reality,
appearing as the sublime Lord Shiva,
lies enthralled beneath the dancing feet
     of the beautiful black Warrior Goddess
who dissolves division and death.

O sisters and brothers,
kindle the sacrificial fire within your hearts.
Pour harmonious and chaotic thoughts
     like clarified butter into these pure flames.
Offer mundane mind as a sacred green leaf
     into the fierce blaze of insight.
This poet immersed in Mother sings:
"Every conflict in my life has been resolved.
Body and mind are possessed by blissful Kali.
With her own hand she inscribes upon this heart
     her declaration of sovereignty."

I move only as you move through me

Essence of awareness! Brilliant Kali!
You are the utterly free play of divine energy.
Every event springs only
    from your sweet will.

You alone act through all our actions,
although we foolishly claim responsibility.
You permit the powerful elephant to sink into quicksand,
the powerless pilgrim to climb the sacred mountain.
You confer upon exalted souls
    a stature as sublime as ruler of the cosmos,
while others you maintain in the most humble station.
Your divine activity remains sheer mystery
    to the singer of this hymn.

I am the instrument, you its adept wielder.
I am the mud-walled village dwelling,
you the tender Mother who abides here.
I am the chariot, you the radiant charioteer.
I move only as you move through me.

This poet calls out, lost in ecstasy:
"O mind, there is nothing more to fear.
I have sold my entire being to the Goddess
    in exchange for her priceless treasure,
the bliss of timeless awareness."

My blissful Mother exists fully through every creature!

Meditate, O mind, on the mystery of Kali.
Use any method of worship you please,
or be free from methods,
breathing day and night her living name
    as the seed of power
planted by the teacher in your heart.

Consider the simple act of lying down to sleep
    as devoted offering of body and mind to her.
Allow your dreams to become
    radiant meditations on the Cosmic Mother.
As you wander through countryside or city,
feel that you are moving through *Kali, Kali, Kali.*
All sounds you hear are her natural mantras
    arising spontaneously
as the whole universe worships her,
prostrates to her, awakens into her.

The Goddess, who is unitive wisdom,
constitutes the letters of every alphabet.
Every word secretly bears the power of her name.

The singer of this mystic hymn is overwhelmed:
"Wonderful! Wonderful! My blissful Mother
    exists fully through every creature!
O wandering poet,
whatever food or drink you receive,
offer as oblation in the sacrificial fire of your body
    and dissolve your mind
into her all-encompassing reality."

There is nothing left but you

Ma! Ma! Ma!
The longing to lose myself in your reality
    burns steadily within me.
My prayer that all beings turn consciously toward you
    remains unwavering and unceasing.
Yet my destiny in this human form is coming to an end
    and you have not responded.
May this be my last breath, O Mother of the Universe,
with which I call fervently to you.

Come now, blissful Mother!
Take my soul in your liberating arms of love!
The world of convention can never know love.
This delirious heart longs to awaken
    into your realm, Ma Kali,
where love is the only reality.

After suffering intensely along the path of desire,
I renounce every selfish craving.
After agonizing over the nature of this momentary world,
I renounce the drive for satisfaction.
After weeping incessantly in fervent prayer,
I can weep no more.

Holy Mother,
my entire being is breaking apart.
There is nothing left but you.

The agony of death will vanish instantly

O foolish tongue, continue to shape
    the sacred sound *Ma Kali, Ma Kali.*
O limited poet, meditate ceaselessly
    on her limitless reality.
Drink from the radiant spring of her name,
fountain of timeless awareness
    for those who truly thirst.

Sisters and brothers, wives and husbands,
teachers and students, daughters and sons,
these most intimate friends will not be
    earthly companions forever, O mind.
At the moment death overcomes the body of the lover,
there remains only the radiant space of Mother.
Call out *Ma Tara, Ma Tara.*
Her name will be ample provision
    for the mysterious journey beyond death
that has already begun.

The cyclic flow of existence is a ceaseless procession
    of events with no abiding reality.
Why do you fail to meditate deeply,
O singer of Mother's heart-melting songs?
Your precious life is wasted in forgetfulness.
Open your eyes and look clearly.
There is Death, standing at your door!

"Dying poses no obstacle, presents no limit,"
this inebriated poet sings.
"Simply utter *Kali, Kali, Kali.*
The agony of death will vanish instantly."

Even the deepest darkness of this world is simply her light!

Will the blessed day ever dawn, O Goddess,
when fiery tears stream from these eyes
      upon uttering your exalted name?
Will subtle obscurations of the mind dissolve,
as this body dances and tumbles on the ground
      in the boundless ecstasy of *Kali, Kali, Kali?*
Will the day of truth finally arrive
      when I cast away every distinction,
free from this and that, here and there?
Will the immense longing of my soul be fulfilled?

Esoteric scriptures of the Goddess declare:
"Ma Tara is utterly formless.
She is clear light beyond all form."
This poet madly responds:
"Mother exists also as each life, every event.
Open your foolish eyes, cease formless meditation,
and perceive the Goddess everywhere!
Even the deepest darkness of this world
      is simply her light!"

I am a child reaching out to catch the moon

Who in the world can know what Mother Kali really is?
She is beyond the reach of every scripture,
every system of philosophy.

As the radiant blackness of divine mystery,
she plays through the lotus wilderness of the sacred human body.
The practitioner of meditation encounters her power
    deep in the blossom of primordial awareness
and within the thousand-petal lotus
    that floats far above the mind.

Kali is the conscious core,
shining through every awakened sage
    who delights in oneness.
This has been demonstrated by countless realized beings.
Ma Tara is the queen of freedom within all hearts.
She reigns timelessly and tenderly.
Planes and dimensions of being
    more vast and subtle than anyone can imagine
are found within her womb of encompassing wisdom.
The Goddess alone knows the extent of her power.
Who else could possibly know?

Laments the singer of this mystic hymn:
"Everyone will laugh at my attempt to swim
    the shoreless sea of her reality,
but my soul belongs to her
    and my heart delights in longing.
I am a child reaching out to catch the moon."

Lost in her paradox, perplexed by her play

O human voice,
you will purify and sanctify your energy
    by intensely chanting *Kali, Kali, Kali*
even for the duration of a single breath.
What reason will remain to fear death?

When the Wisdom Goddess is awakened
    by sweetly singing her name
in the luminous cave of the heart,
what motive can remain to offer flowers,
to tell beads, to make pilgrimage?
Why should one who experiences all as Mother
    perform finite worship?
Who is there to meditate on whom?

Yet the singer of this strange song still feels
    deep longing to visit and meet with her,
and my drive for liberation from the mundane world
    remains constantly clear.

Offering red blossoms at her dark feet,
I am crying *Why? Why? Why?*
This poet of the Great Goddess
    is lost in her paradox,
perplexed by her play.

Sing ceaselessly the name of Kali

O human mind, while thinking and perceiving,
invoke instinctively the subtle sound *Om Kali.*
Why not ground your entire being in her living name
    that dissolves all dangers arising
from without and from within?
How can you forget, even for an instant,
the innate cry *Ma! Ma! Ma!*
    that resounds throughout the worlds?
While facing the terrible expanse of universal suffering,
the mind that remembers Mother experiences no fear.
The boundless power of Kali
    will carry the mind effortlessly
across the stormy sea of birth and death.

O mundane mind,
stop thinking in habitual patterns,
move beyond the structure of past, present, future,
leave your obsession with temporality.
Without care or regret sing *Ma Tara, Ma Kali.*
Sail smoothly across the ocean of relativity.

Overcome with fervent love, this poet pleads:
"O mind, how can you possibly forget the Goddess?
At the very center of your being
    sing ceaselessly the name of Kali
and drink her deathless nectar.
Your life in the deceptive current of time
    is coming to an end.
Soon you will know only Mother."

Unveil the self-radiant diamond of your essence

O distracted mind,
why are you indulging in anxiety?
Be still for just the space of *Kali, Kali, Kali*
    and concentrate your gaze on her reality.
Those who worship the Goddess with splendid ceremony
    become imbued with pride.
Much better is the inward path of secret devotion,
invisible to the curious stare of the world.

Why construct static images of Mother Reality
    from metal, stone, straw, clay?
Allow pure mind to compose her form
    from consciousness alone.
Place this living image on the heart lotus
    and wait for her to come.

Why bother to gather ripe plantains
    to present with ritual gestures at her feet?
She delights only in the nectar of selfless love,
offered directly and abundantly,
breath by breath.

Why worship with such profusion of jewels and lamps?
Unveil the self-radiant diamond of your essence,
O mind, and allow it alone to illuminate
    the heart's secret shrine day and night.

What sense is there to sacrifice animals
    as worship of Goddess Kali,
when she desires only the death of egocentricity?
Cut through these childish dreams of separation
    with her sword of nondual wisdom,
crying: "Victory to Kali! *Jai Ma Kali!*
May your truth of oneness triumph endlessly!"

The singer of this hymn has no need for flute or drum
    but calls ecstatically to everyone:
"Clap your hands and proclaim melodiously
    Ma Kali's universal victory,
until the mind dissolves completely
    into her inconceivable reality."

Beat the great drum of fearlessness

O longing mind,
focus all your longing on Mother Kali.
You will receive pure love and liberating knowledge
    tangibly as fruits placed on the palm of the hand.
Release any lingering pride of personal power
    and merge your entire being with her.
This is the worship that disappoints Death.

Please heed the call of Mother Reality!
Inwardly repeat Kali's transforming name
    and discover the fountain of illumination
where the thirst of her lovers is quenched,
their very being immersed in her being.

Infused by Goddess Wisdom,
this poet proclaims with adamantine conviction:
"Sisters and brothers, release your root obsession,
your greed, anger, pride, jealousy.
These are only forms of fear.
Beat the great drum of fearlessness
    and reach the final goal,
awakening as pure consciousness."

This poet longs to love, not to disappear

What sense is there to wander away on pilgrimage?
All sacred places exist only here at Mother's feet.
I can swim in the timeless ocean of bliss
    by evoking her presence in the heart lotus.
Why travel? Why search?
The dancing feet of Kali are vast red blossoms.
Each petal contains a powerful place of pilgrimage.

Every obscurity of mind and heart is cleared
    by the subtle sound *Om Kali.*
Mountains of cotton are consumed instantly by fire.
If the head is gone, can the headache remain?
When the entire being is lost
    in the open space of Kali,
can there be any impure thought or activity?

Traditional religion teaches that debts to ancestral spirits
    are cleared by traveling great distances
to offer ceremonial rice.
Someone intimate with Goddess Kali
    can only laugh at this troublesome journey.

Shiva teaches that dying in the sacred city of Benares
    liberates the soul from bondage,
but devotion to Mother Reality
    illuminates those who are still living.
His liberating knowledge is servant to her ecstatic love,
Shiva's breast the dancing ground for *Kali, Kali, Kali.*

O mind, consider carefully.
What attraction can there be in the notion of nirvana?
Why would the soul wish to become a raindrop
    that melts into an infinite ocean?
Can one appreciate the delicate sweetness of sugar
    by becoming an inert crystal of sugar

or even a mountain of sugar?
This poet longs to love, not to disappear.

Mind whirling with bewilderment and awe,
the singer of this mystic hymn exclaims:
"I exist only through the grace and power of Mother.
Simply the vision of her tangled hair,
streaming wildly as she dances,
confers the four fruits of highest aspiration:
righteousness, abundance, delight,
and total illumination."

Why do you continue to test my soul?

O Kali of Mystery!
I yearn to hold your luminous power
    in the subtle nerve channels near the spine
long enough to know you more intensely.
Yet your brilliant Goddess energy
    dances with freedom and wild abandon.
How can I possibly contain you, even for an instant?
May you come to rest gently
    upon the spacious lotus of my heart,
playing with pure awareness
    the many-stringed instrument of my mind.

O longing soul,
this poet will tell you
    how to embrace Mother's feet of bliss.
Cut through veils of greed, anger, pride, and jealousy
    with her sword of nonduality.
Dedicate your life to her indivisible presence.
By singing her name with passion,
transform your being into a full expression of her being.
This will utterly ruin Death's reputation
    and free you from limits forever.

The singer of this song complains:
"Mother! Mother! Mother!
Why do you continue to test my soul
    with the suffering of this provisional world?
What more can I dedicate, sacrifice, release?
But do whatever you will with me.
I will continue to accept the play of daily life
    as your most precious teaching,
never ceasing to sing
    Kali, Kali, Kali."

You will discover a new gem every moment

O desperately seeking mind,
invoke the primal resonance *Kali, Kali, Kali*
      and plunge into the ocean of her reality.
Do not imagine this transparent sea to be empty
      if you fail to discover living gems
during the first few dives.
Sink deep with a single breath,
awakening her energy that abides secretly
      within this precious human body.
The priceless pearl of love is manifest
      only at the uttermost depth
of Mother's wisdom ocean.

O aspiring mind,
seek the Goddess with intense devotion,
following initiation and instruction from Shiva.
You will certainly encounter her
      and become her.

Greed, anger, pride, and jealousy
      are gigantic crocodiles,
swimming in the ocean of Goddess Kali,
inhabiting the shallows of relativity.
Rub your body with the pungent herb,
renunciation of egocentricity.
The hungry predators will never touch you
      when they smell this burning fragrance.

Treasures of revelation
      emerge from the Mother ocean,
from unthinkable profundity.
This courageous poet confirms:
"Dive with abandon into her mystery.
You will discover a new gem every moment."

Wherever I go there is only Kali

Ceaselessly resonating with her sound,
wherever I go there is only *Kali, Kali, Kali.*
Her lovers are liberated and illuminated
    during this very lifetime
under all conditions of consciousness.

My beloved human guide, ocean of mercy,
selfless friend of all who seek refuge,
showed me the bright wisdom feet of the Goddess
    dancing and shining in my heart,
revealing her as the vast tree of enlightenment
    rooted in the center of awareness,
fulfilling the deepest aspiration of all living beings.

Through the holy companionship of my mentor,
the Mother of the Universe has come to dwell in my home
    as brilliant Goddess Lakshmi,
overflowing fountain of abundance.
Mother abides now in my voice as subtle Saraswati,
sweet singer of radical wisdom.
Through the blessing of my spiritual friend,
the knowledge of Shiva and the power of Tara
    guide and protect me night and day.

The ascetic who practices in remote solitude
    desires to be unified with formless radiance,
while the worldly person craves
    the constant diversion of earthly pleasure.
Children of the Wisdom Mother
    are never caught in this dichotomy.
She grants freely to her ecstatic devotee
    the delight of earth and the bliss of union.
Both are her reality.

Flooded with rapture, this poet sings:
"Lovers of Goddess Kali
    are successful on every level.
They are granted supernatural powers
    known only to advanced practitioners
and leave even these behind."

Please bring my poems with you

O my lazy mind,
clearly you do not know how to farm.
You allow your own fertile expanse to lie fallow.
Under proper cultivation, the land of awareness
        becomes golden with the harvest of illumination.
Sow seeds with every breath.
Protect the precious field of your soul
        with the fence of Mother Kali's name,
so the fruit of your dedicated effort
        will not be stolen by the egocentric world.

Impenetrable is the fiery fence *Kali! Kali! Kali!*
Even Death dares not approach it.
Be utterly confident, O simpleminded poet.
Encircled by this powerful resonance,
your meditations in song will remain fruitful
        for many hundred years.

The soul is the field of free decision.
Dedicate yourself to constant cultivation
        for the sake of all conscious beings,
and the harvest will be without limit.
Your spiritual guide has given you
        the mystic syllable of Mother essence
as potent seed to sow.
Water for irrigation flows abundantly through the heart
        as pure love and tender devotion.

This dusty troubadour
        wandering through open fields
now pleads with everyone:
"If you find farming difficult,
please bring my poems with you."

Vast harvest of illumination for all living beings

O Wisdom Goddess,
may I cultivate this open field of awareness
    throughout my precious lifetime.
O Mother of the Universe,
shower your grace upon this black and fertile soil!
Be pleased with my intense longing!

Ma! Ma! Ma!
Mundane consciousness is choked with weeds.
How can I till the entire expanse of body and mind?
If I can clear and cultivate even a small section,
my jubilation will know no boundary.
Thorny brambles of negative thoughts and actions
    continue to spring from the soil of the heart.
O Warrior Goddess with streaming black hair,
one swing from your sword of wisdom
    will cut every egocentric root
and clarify this heart forever.

I will tame the primal obsessions,
greed, anger, pride, hatred,
and use them as powerful bullocks
    to plow the field of consciousness.
Sowing the seed of *Om Kali Ma,*
transmitted to me by a skillful farmer,
I will reap a vast harvest
    of illumination for all living beings.

This useless poet laments:
"My commitment to tilling the ground of my being
    is neither consistent nor deep.
Yet how intensely I long, O Mother,
to taste your most intimate presence,
to merge my soul with the radiance
    of your dark blue wisdom feet!"

Listen to me, Death!

Listen to me, Death!
You must leave here immediately.
How can you touch me?
I have captured Goddess Kali.
I have bound her hands and feet
    with adamantine strands of pure love.
Her intimate presence alone
    now shines from the stronghold of my heart.
The twelve-petal lotus that floats in my chest
    is surrounded by her fierce flames.

I contemplate with awe
    the thousand-petal lotus at my crown
where the golden honey of mystic union
    is flowing eternally.
O Mother Kundalini,
my entire being is swept upward continuously
    by your current of wisdom energy.

I have taken precautions so that Goddess Kali
    cannot escape from within me.
Single-minded devotion guards her with every breath.
These two eyes are her gatekeepers.
My third eye has become her own clear vision.

Suspecting that the fatal fever of egocentricity
    would attack my mind and body,
I have taken the ancient remedy
    prescribed by my illumined master.
The medicine *Om Kali,* taken four times daily,
cures the chronic illness of *me! me! me!*

Emboldened by the indwelling of the Mother,
this warrior poet calls out:
"Listen to me, Death, so your insane pride

will at last be humbled.
You can take away only this form.
I have already begun my deathless journey,
chanting *Kali! Kali! Kali!*"

I throw the dust of pure devotion into the eyes of Death

Watch closely, Death!
I am now standing with my entire being
    grounded in Mother Reality.
I am drawing a fiery boundary
    with the living name of Kali.
I challenge you to cross.

I tell you, Death,
I am no premature infant of the Wisdom Mother
    whom you can threaten to overpower!
You cannot snatch me away
    like candy from the hands of a child
who is reduced to terror by your empty threat.
If you address one harsh word to me, Death,
you will be confronted by my terrible Mother.
Goddess Kali is the beloved destroyer.
Her furious bliss that obliterates every limit
    terrorizes even Death.

Her playful poet sings:
"Fearlessly celebrating the beauty of Ma Kali,
I throw the dust of pure devotion
    into the eyes of Death
and easily elude its clumsy grasp."

Could a foolish poet grasp her mystery?

Wait awhile longer, Death.
I am singing to Mother
    about my longing to return into her.
She will come very soon
    to dissolve the anguish
of this conventional world.

Be patient, Death.
You will inevitably take my body,
but do not expect me to fear you abjectly.
Around my neck I wear the amulet of Tara's name
    and the fragrant garland of her living presence.
The Mother of the Universe is my queen
    and I am subject only to her.
Sometimes I am swept along by the current of distress,
other times I swim in the calm sea of abundance.
Under every condition, she sustains me.

The singer of this strange song can only cry:
"All experience is the elusive play of Mother,
impossible for the mind to comprehend.
Could a foolish poet grasp her mystery
    that eludes even Lord Shiva,
who is clear knowledge of ultimacy?"

Dissolving the demons of egocentricity

Stop and consider carefully!
Is the Mother of the Universe
    conceivable by the human mind?
Is she a subject of philosophy or theology?
Her mysterious name of power,
    Ma Kali, Ma Kali,
is repeated even by transcendent Reality,
allowing sublime Lord Shiva
    to consume the poisonous negativity
constantly arising in the hearts of countless beings.

The insubstantial process,
creation, preservation, and dissolution,
occurs through a single glance from her eye of power.
This universe, with its endless dimensions,
exists only within her luminous womb of power.
Now can you sense how vast she is?

Taking refuge in Mother's guidance,
even heavenly beings are saved from subtle dangers,
and Shiva, ground and essence of divinity,
lies lost in formless ecstasy
    beneath her dancing feet of power.

The singer of this mystic hymn is overwhelmed
    by the sudden vision of Kali
as supreme Warrior of Wisdom,
roaming the battleground of universal suffering,
dissolving the demons of egocentricity
    with her terrible cry of power.

Please sever with your brilliant sword of wisdom

Mother! Mother! Mother!
I labor long hours in the marketplace
    of habit and convention.
I am the employee of a ghost,
without even a few coins of wisdom.
I am a public porter, bearing upon my head
    nothing but concepts and projects
that bring no recompense.
I work intensely night and day,
yet whatever I accumulate is consumed instantly
    by the hungry play of energy,
earth, air, fire, water, space.

The five elements are constantly quarreling
    with the six passions
and the ten organs of perception and action.
I try to intervene, but they are fond of war,
deaf to every counsel of peace.
Ma! Ma! Ma!
I cannot bear this mundane existence
    for many more moments.
As blind beggar drops precious staff,
finds it again, and holds it with intense gratitude,
so I long to hold your abiding presence
    at the center of awareness.
Yet my mind forgets Mother at almost every breath
    because of its prolonged history
of carelessness and death.

This desperate poet prays:
"O Mother of the Universe,
please sever with your brilliant sword of wisdom
    the bonds of egocentric thought and action,

and allow my soul's light to rise
    through the crown of my head,
the gateway to total illumination."

Simply abide at the primal root of awareness

O simple mind, listen carefully.
You are my tame bird.
I am training you to repeat the name of Kali.
Heed the wise proverb,
whoever learns a lesson thoroughly
lives perfectly content.
Whenever you become dull, O mind,
remember the common adage,
the student who shuns study
will be beaten soundly.

O foolish mind, sing *Kali, Kali, Kali.*
You will experience sheer delight
at her feet of mystery.
When your body and the whole universe
resound with her name,
you will taste everywhere the sweetness
of your own pure essence,
and attain liberation now.

O mind, strange winging creature,
why continue to fly here and there?
How many years can you survive
on meager crumbs of convention?
Listen to my heartfelt plea!
Seek from your own true nature
the four fruits of highest aspiration:
righteousness, power, delight, illumination.

Tears of love flowing abundantly,
Mother's poet invites all humanity:
"Partake freely of this radiant fruit
from the tree of divine energy.

Simply abide at the primal root of awareness
   and shake its branches
with the innate cry *Om Kali, Om Kali.*"

Pay no heed to narrow-minded persons

O mind that by its very nature
    plunges into ecstasy,
be still and listen.
Pay no heed to narrow-minded persons
    who call you drunk or mad.
How can they know that you imbibe
    the nectar of timeless awareness,
not mundane intoxicants?

Today my whole being is so sweetly reeling
    with Mother's own drunken love
that even those soaked in ordinary wine
    consider me one of them!
O sisters and brothers,
please abide night and day in ecstasy
    beneath the red-soled feet
that delight even Absolute Reality,
or you will be disoriented
    by the wine of egocentric pleasure.

The luminous egg of this cosmos
    floats on the elixir of ecstatic love
that flows from the sound of Mother Kali's name.
She lifts hearts from the common birth of selfishness
    to the noble rank of selfless lovers.
Never abandon the life of dedication to Kali,
O lovers of her reality,
simply because the world of convention
    cannot accept your intense ecstasy.

The world tapestry is woven from three strands:
inertia, balance, and dynamic energy.
These alone are the mundane intoxicants.
From the strand of balance
    comes self-serving intelligence,

from energy ambitious action,
from inertia ignorance.
Drawn sharply between these three,
your soul's instrument falls out of harmony.
Only the Divine Troubadour can tune you again
    with her strong and skillful hands.

From her the poet now receives these lines:
"Never allow the world's opinion
    to dim the delight of nonduality,
nor draw you away even subtly
    from Mother's wonderful intimacy."

I have received the clear order that Death must die

From the Mother of the Universe,
whose divine authority is absolute,
I have received the clear order that Death must die.

The supreme Warrior of Wisdom
    sends me the potent gift of her name,
her self-directing arrow
    that I bear in the quiver of my heart,
keeping it keen by constant chanting.
This mystic arrow has already been victorious
    over the notions *me* and *mine,*
common intruders who steal away
    with the treasure of selfless devotion.
Now Death must be killed,
leaving the entire field of battle empty.
There is nothing more important
    than this profound duty,
the root transformation of humanity.

The radiant hero Rama conquered
    the central stronghold of negation
simply by offering blue flowers at Mother's feet.
I now offer her the seven subtle lotus centers
    of the pristine spiritual body,
and the booming drum of realization
    at once announces the conquest of mortality.

This poet requests everyone to consider carefully:
"Why should we strive to dedicate our whole being
    to the source and matrix of being?
Because by failing to take refuge consciously
    in timeless Mother Reality,
we would give ourselves instead
    to the pervasive illusion of dying."

Consecrate your being to pure love

O longing mind,
consecrate your being to pure love.
Turn every thought to Goddess Tara.
She will bear you tenderly across the raging sea
    of separation and individuality.

Be utterly dedicated to her reality.
Cry aloud *Ma Kali, Ma Kali.*
Know that she can clarify
    the inconceivable maze of relativity.
To hope for assistance and guidance through this world
    from wealth, relatives, and religious rites
provides no profound solution.
Have you forgotten that everyone is lost?

Where are you now? Why are you traveling?
This cosmos is the strange theater where souls act,
wearing various costumes and disguises.
This intricate play of transparent energy
    is initiated, sustained, and dissolved by Kali,
who is the dream power of Absolute Reality.
At this very moment, you are resting
    on the vast lap of Mother's cosmic dream
that you misperceive
    as the narrow prison of suffering.
Why abandon the kingdom of awareness
    to obsession with self and disdain for others,
to hollow passion and abject clinging?
You are creating a disease without a remedy.
The brief day of your earthly life is almost over.
Meditate now on beautiful Black Tara.
She is seated upon the jewel island of essence
    in the transparent sea of ultimacy.

This poet sings drunkenly:
"Tara! Tara! Tara!
Your name is ambrosia.
May all beings enter the secret sanctuary
    through your name,
tasting the unique sweetness
    of self-luminous awareness."

This poet knows truth directly as Mother!

Take care, my intimate friend.
Become aware!
The boat of your body is sinking
    into the sea of cosmic energy.
O careless mind,
the fleeting day of your conventional life
    is disappearing into twilight,
and still you do not remember ceaselessly
    the Goddess who delights Absolute Reality.

You filled your vessel with heavy freight,
acquired on the black market
    of egocentric desiring.
You wasted your daylight hours
    gossiping at the boat landing,
setting sail only when surprised by dusk.

Your ship is weather-beaten by worldliness.
Negative thoughts and actions
    have opened long cracks along its hull.
Your only chance to cross
    the ocean of delusion
is to invite the noble Wisdom Goddess
    to stand watch at your helm,
or else the six oarsmen, mind and senses,
will become paralyzed
    by the sight of Death's huge waves.

O sisters and brothers,
dedicate your entire being to truth,
to the light of ultimacy
    that shines through your own humanity.
This poet knows truth directly
    as Mother! Mother! Mother!

During deep meditation, I no longer encounter I

O you who liberate! You who illuminate!
Please free your child from this persistent fantasy
    of being a limited mind and body
that are born and that die repeatedly.

Ma! Ma! Ma!
I am overwhelmed by the relentless suffering
    within these mental and physical realms.
Ma Kali, please do not allow me
    to weep endlessly.
As Warrior Goddess of unitive wisdom,
you destroy egocentric separation.
Please, Mother, cut through the misery
    of the careless child who sings this song.

No longer will I be fooled
    by the alluring fruits of selfish motivation,
knowing them to lack true sweetness.
Such false delicacies are filled with subtle poison
    that devastates consciousness.
Partaking of them, we lose spiritual sensitivity.
Most tender Tara, I do not want to forget you
    even for a single heartbeat.
You are my mother, my matrix, my bliss.
Great Goddess, please do not allow me
    to consume negativity.

The fruits of mundane existence drive me insane,
causing me to claim this universe as mine alone,
my loved ones, my sense organs, mine, all mine!
But where is the possessive ego to be found?
During deep meditation, I no longer encounter I.

This awakened poet can only cry:
"Blissful Mother, please lead all humanity
    on the mystic way, unveiling your identity.
You alone are real.
Do not keep your lovers
    wandering in the illusion
of division and limitation.

What gift can I offer you?

Mother of Infinity,
what gift can I offer you?
Plunging deep into meditation,
I perceive all lives and worlds are yours alone.
Why should your lovers present you
    with necklaces of gems and garments of silk?
The universe is a boundless ocean of jewels
    that humbly touches your feet,
the blackness between stars your only covering.
You are the mountain of inexhaustible abundance.
You reign over the golden city of truth.
Compared with your divine wealth,
even the Absolute appears as a wandering beggar
    clothed only in open space.

Contemplating my elusive Mother,
this poet is overwhelmed with ecstasy
    and inquires again and again:
"Who is she? Who is she?
At her uncrossable threshold of mystery
    the Creator and Preserver of the universe
stands in awe and supplication."

Who can comprehend your countless revelations?

Mother of Ultimacy,
unspeakable and unthinkable,
who can comprehend your countless revelations?

Sometimes you appear as the peaceful helpmate
    seated beside Shiva in quiet harmony,
other times you dance with warrior's ecstasy
    on the vast breast of Absolute Reality.
Sometimes you manifest as the radiant cosmos
    and its countless living beings,
other times you reveal yourself as the Mystic Woman,
solitary and magnificent in her true nakedness.
Sometimes you play as incomparable Radha,
courageous lover of Lord Krishna,
other times you become dark blue Krishna,
Divine Love who falls in rapture
    at Radha's golden feet.

Sometimes you remove every veil
    to be known by enlightened sages
as the formless Mother of the Universe,
the transparent presence who dwells secretly
    within every atom, every perception, every event.
Other times you manifest as Mother Kundalini,
the evolutionary potency
    coiled at the root of the subtle body.

This mad poet refuses to pay heed
    to any theology, any philosophy.
I can only weep:
"Ma! Ma! Ma!
This is your sweetest name,
transcending all descriptions.
Mother, allow me always to call you *Mother.*
Keep me forever at your dark blue wisdom feet."

Do what you will with me!

O mind, my ancient friend,
this projected universe
    is only the faint reflection of reality.
By attempting to grasp reflected images,
we cheat ourselves of true experience.
Turn instead to the original,
and discover the limitless treasure of delight.

This realm of reflection we encounter
    consists of mind, earth, wind, fire, water,
arranging and rearranging with increasing complexity.
The principle of subtle energy
    evolves naturally into tangibility,
blossoming as living worlds beyond number.
A single sun reflects in countless water-bearing vessels.
As these earthenware worlds are broken, one by one,
the sunlight of primal awareness remains the same.

Floating in the Cosmic Mother's lucent womb,
we are all contemplatives,
but taking birth in the obscure realm of separation,
we consume earth instead of nectar,
convention instead of rapture,
time instead of timelessness.
The cord that bound me to my human mother
    was severed quickly and cleanly by the midwife.
Can I cut as easily this illusion of bondage to the world?

The passionate words of a selfish lover
    at first taste sweeter than honey,
but they contain the poison of delusion.
The singer of this song once drained
    the cup of selfish love
and felt the anguish of its touch.

But now Mother's poet tastes only her authentic bliss
    and weeps with spiritual tears:
"Ma Kali! Ma Kali! Ma Kali!
Great Goddess! Union of relative and absolute!
Laughing daughter of the eternal snow mountain!
Do what you will with me!"

The enlightenment of the whole being

My cherished poet friend,
please bring your mind
      to the exalted level of the heart's sincerity.
There are countless yogis who wander about
      displaying the external marks of sanctity,
but their private thought and action
      run counter to their pious teaching,
though hair and beard may be
      long as the hanging roots of the banyan tree.

My foolish friend, listen carefully.
If Lord Shiva, who is Absolute Reality,
can be realized by worshiping natural images of stone,
why not adore stone mountains ceaselessly
      by night and by day?
If you imagine that Mother Kali's wisdom feet
      can be experienced by sitting with closed eyes,
why are all blind persons not illumined sages?

This chastened poet sings to everyone:
"Please pray to Mother to transform your mind
      with the delicate light of the heart's sincerity.
With this pure mind, practice
      the meditation beyond all meditation.
You will attain final success in spiritual life,
the enlightenment of the whole being,
including all its passionate intensity."

White ants of selfish desire

Mother of the Universe,
what else will you display to me
    during this chaotic lifetime?
My soul's journey across the planetary plane
    bears no sweet spiritual fruit.
Even though I am a child of the Universal Mother,
the house of this body is now barely habitable.

My human form was a simple dwelling,
O Mother, though beautifully designed.
But now it has become choked by vines of old age,
haunted by ghosts of disease and death.
Many monsoon seasons of habitual thought and perception
    have dampened these earthen walls,
and now they are disintegrating.
White ants of selfish desire
    are chewing through my thatched roof.

Utterly disillusioned by the world of convention,
this poet prays with revolutionary fervor:
"Ma Tara! Ma Tara!
You who bring the soul to truth!
You who pour awareness
    into pure awareness!
What shall I do? Where shall I go?
I cannot bear to build
    another home for separate ego."

Why remain in deep depression?

O mind, why remain in deep depression
    as though you were a motherless child?
Always remember: *I have a Mother.*

Since your Mother is queen of the universe,
how can you fear the power of death?
Your anxiety over dying, O mind, is like a serpent
    who lives in constant terror of a frog.
Surely this is the strangest of delusions.

As beloved child of the Universal Mother,
you can and must be utterly fearless.
Fear of death is plain insanity.
Your Mother is supreme sovereign.
There is no one and nothing you can fear,
for nothing and no one exist apart from her.
Why indulge any longer in despondency?
Ceaselessly sing *Kali! Kali! Kali!*
She will awaken you to nonduality.

This spiritually born child of the Goddess
    aspires wholeheartedly:
"May my mind become radiantly pure,
and with this mind of purity may I meditate
    upon the mystic seed sound *Ma,*
entrusted to me by my Cosmic Mother."

O childish mind, meditate this way,
merging ever more deeply with her reality.
Death and life are simply her play.

Turn around and rectify your basic error

O mind, pay clear attention.
Turn around and rectify your basic error.
You imagine that you have lost your point of origin,
and you wander about desperately seeking
    what is already the root of your own being.

The path to the original source
    is ecstatic love.
Consider how intensely you love
    your most intimate companions
and direct that much tender feeling
    toward the Mother of the Universe,
who is pure awareness.

Your body is a crystalline structure,
its atoms like diamonds.
When these atomic patterns separate,
the body is destroyed.
Can any structure in the universe exist
    as separate individuality?
Contemplate deeply! Discover nonduality!
There is only Mother Reality!

The singer of this gnostic hymn declares:
"My Mother, source of creativity,
expresses fully through all her creatures,
moving about subtly, secretly, and blissfully
    within her own essentiality."

Why disappear into formless trance?

O wavering mind,
awaken your upward-flowing awareness.
Become the sublime warrior Goddess Kali,
who moves with graceful power
    through the vast landscape of the body.

Her divine form, like a black storm cloud
    illumined by the sun,
she stands unveiled,
her long hair falling free like monsoon rain.
Be lost in awe of her, O mind,
for you will never comprehend her.

She dwells as the primal lotus of conscious energy
    and also as the thousand-petal blossom,
complete enlightenment.
She is none other than primordial bliss,
this great swan ever swimming
    through the lotus jungle of the subtle body.

Gaze intently into the blazing heart of joy
    and you will perceive my blissful Mother,
matrix of all phenomena.
The vision of Kali
    kindles the fire of unitive wisdom,
burning down conventional barriers,
pervading minds and worlds with light,
revealing her exalted beauty
    as universal flower garden
and universal cremation ground,
where lovers merge with Mother Reality,
experiencing the single taste of nonduality.

This ardent poet of the Goddess cries:
"Every lover longs only
    to gaze upon the unique Beloved.
Why close your eyes?
Why disappear into formless trance?"

I am always within light

Mother of the Universe,
what do you encounter in your own meditation?

Mother of Wisdom, you gaze effortlessly
    through the insubstantial veil of relativity,
but consider the predicament of the devotee
    who is now crying out to you.
Whenever my flickering lamp of meditative practice
    is temporarily extinguished,
my opponents, the countless egocentric impulses,
laugh and dance in triumph.

Even though there is oil of devotion
    and the wick of concentration is trimmed,
my lamp is constantly in danger of being smothered
    by the swarming beetles of selfish desire.
These peculiar and elusive insects puzzle me.
They seem to appear from nowhere.

Yet this helpless child of Mother
    is protected even from subtle danger
and sings with joyous release:
"Ma! Ma! Ma!
You have revealed the revolutionary truth.
Regardless of this uncertain lamp,
this inconsistent contemplation,
my essential nature is already light.
I am always within light, O Mother,
always returning home to light.
When these physical eyes close for the last time,
darkness will dissolve into light
    and light into you."

Who can keep a blazing fire tied in a cotton cloth?

My intimate companion,
why not plunge into union
    with Great Goddess Kali?
Discover your spiritual anxiety
    to be without the slightest ground.

The obscure night of your religious quest is over
    and the day of truth is dawning.
The sunlight of Mother Wisdom instantly pervades
    the landscape of awareness,
for darkness is not a substance that offers resistance.
Precious Kali, you have risen as the morning sun,
opening the lotus centers of my subtle perception
    to your naked, timeless radiance.

Proliferating systems of ritual and philosophy
    attempt to throw dust into the eyes
of the eternal wisdom that abides in every soul.
How can any system transcend the play of relativity?
But when relative existence is revealed
    as the country fair of Mother's sheer delight,
there are no teachers and nothing to teach,
no students and nothing to learn.
The actors and their lines are simply expressions
    of the Wisdom Goddess
who directs this entire drama.
Be confident that you will soon awaken fully
    as the essence of her reality!

The courageous lover tastes the bliss of the Beloved
    and enters the secret city of the Goddess,
passing beyond the threshold of ecstasy
    into the open expanse of enlightenment.

Astonished by this sudden journey,
Mother's poet now sings madly:
"My delusion is gone, gone, utterly gone!
Who can obscure truth?
Who can keep a blazing fire tied in a cotton cloth?"

I refuse to sing your praises any longer!

Ma Kali, you have been so unkind to me!
I refuse to sing your praises any longer!

You are indeed the Wisdom Woman,
sublime feminine principle who wields so freely
    her flashing sword of nonduality,
cutting away both subjectivity and objectivity.
As naked truth, you dance magnificently,
alone on the empty battlefield of relativity,
smiling mysteriously, glowing eyes gazing inwardly.

Yet even your irresistible power
    could not protect your helpless lover,
and now I have lost my means of livelihood.
You are without any question the Mother of Wisdom,
but you have given this child a head with no brain.

Your poor poet, soon to be destitute,
can only cry in consternation:
"Ma! Ma! Ma!
What have you done to me during this lifetime?
You loaded a leaky boat
    with the heavy treasure of your name
and allowed it to sink in the waters of worldliness.
Not only has my venture reaped no profit,
my entire savings have been lost."

I reside in the mystical court of the Black Queen

I am living in the mysterious kingdom of merciful Kali.
I am her direct representative, she my exalted sovereign.
Beware, Death, you have no idea who I am!
When you recognize me, you will be terrified.

I reside in the mystical court of the Black Queen,
bearing the silken pillow for her feet of radiance.
I am her intimate attendant, she my supreme beloved.
My life's essence is her beautiful estate,
never ravaged by flood, torn by conflict,
turned to dust by drought, decimated by disease.
Her ambrosial name flows through this endless land,
a sacred river, its clear water ecstasy,
its bed the bright sand of purity.

This eternal companion of Goddess Kali
    is filled with courage and cries fearlessly:
"O foolish Death,
you exist as an insubstantial specter,
terrifying only to those who are immature.
You cannot imagine
    the secret nature of Her Majesty,
who has granted you such a humble function
    in her boundless kingdom."

Sail with me! Sail with me!

O mind that wanders
    through this momentary world,
the transcendental vessel of Goddess Tara
    has cast anchor in the harbor.
Come swiftly if you wish to board the wondrous ship
    that bears souls to the truth.
Untie the complex mental knots
    that moor you to the mundane realm.
Unfurl the bright sail *Tara, Tara, Tara.*
Ply with vigor the oars of contemplation
    if you wish to set sail
and cross the stormy ocean of delusion.

Stop purchasing cheap experiences
    from the bazaar of habit and convention.
Cease this aimless browsing.
Your brief day of earthly life is almost over,
leaving you only the fleeting hours
    of twilight and evening.
What more can you learn from bartering and bickering
    in the marketplace of desire?

This avid voyager of the Mother sings:
"Courage! Courage! Be courageous!
Sail with me! Sail with me!
Break free forever from imaginary bondage,
from selfish grasping, from separate individuality!"

The diamond essence of awareness

Ma Tara, you are truly the exalted one,
the essence of awareness.
But are you aware of the foolish poet
    who sings this song?
You are indeed the radiant truth,
the sun that dissolves like morning mist
    the illusory suffering of conscious beings.
But what about my persistent misery?

Revelatory experience flows to devout practitioners
    from the Mother of the Universe,
but consider what Mother bestows on me.
During morning meditation, I worry about livelihood.
At noon prayer, I think about delicious food.
While practicing contemplation in the evening,
my mind wanders at random among events of the day.

Goddess Tara, I ask you frankly,
will you ever allow this distracted consciousness
    any sustained vision of your reality?
The only visionary gift granted me
    is the viewpoint of arbitrary convention.
In this fascinating vision, I am constantly absorbed.

The deeper I plunge into thought,
the more I realize I cannot know you by thinking,
O blissful Mother, beyond speech and mind.

This desperate seeker of truth cries out:
"*Ma! Ma! Ma!*
Daughter of the mystic mountain!
You dance, holding the brilliant gem of realization.
But when I try to grasp
    the diamond essence of awareness,
it appears to turn back into common stone."

Gaze into your own original face!

Mother! Mother! Mother!
Your dream-play universe is sheer delight.
Souls caught in the seriousness of your drama
    are constantly running, looking for release.
The egocentric bind themselves,
mindlessly repeating: *this is I, that is mine.*
But souls who know their own boundless nature
    are free and happy under every condition.

O my childish mind,
you assume Mother's display of names and forms
    to be substantial and real,
participating with such anxiety and self-importance.
What are these objects and opinions
    you claim to dominate and to possess?
What is this self you imagine yourself to be?
What exists apart from the timeless awareness
    that is the core of all experience?
O mind, who is there to worship whom?
Joy and sorrow are simply Mother Kali's play.
Neither is her reality.

Kindling the bright light of nondual wisdom
    within the dark room of mere convention,
discover the treasure of essence
    and conceal it in the heart without a trace.
Refusing to play a role in the drama of religion,
carefully put out the light again.

This poet, intoxicated by stealing away with truth,
cries out to every unique seeker of truth:
"Now lift the curtain of relative existence
    and gaze into your own original face!"

You have forgotten your essence

O mind, you have forgotten your essence
    and are lost in relentless speculation.
Day and night, you imagine finding
    somewhere within relative existence
a cache of precious coins,
a brilliant solution to cyclic sorrow,
but every coin of this mundane realm
    is worthless counterfeit.

Mother Wisdom alone is pure gold,
the only treasure,
yet you barter her golden radiance
    at the very center of your being
for a fragmentary world of mere colored glass.

O my idiotic mind,
what misfortune you have brought upon yourself!
No one reaps a rich harvest of insight
    who has not sown seeds of selflessness.
The principle of action and its fruit
    is incontrovertible.
You wander here and there, O mind,
remaining confined by the field of destiny
    that you yourself have fenced and cultivated.

Time exists only through the mind,
spreading inexorably like the tendrils
    of some vast undergrowth.
Singing *Kali, Kali, Kali*
    with breath become pure and selfless,
practice her contemplation and cut time down
    with the sword of nonduality.

This poet challenges humanity:
"How can you think clearly or kindly?

You have become a beast of burden,
bridled, saddled, and ridden
    by senses, passions, mental faculties.
Each rider wants to take a different way.
How can you hope to reach
    the evolutionary goal,
conscious union with her reality?"

My entire being shining with your name

Who can fathom the judgments
    handed down by the Mother of the Universe?
Though repeating day and night her name of power,
this poet of the Mother still faces the sentence of death.
I humbly submit to you, O Goddess,
my petition for immediate release.
Free from all diversion,
awaiting only your decision,
my palms touch constantly in prayer.
When will my case be heard before the highest court
    where you alone preside?

My mind is lacking purity and clarity.
Will I have the strength to bear your examination,
to answer all your questions truly?
Will I receive your tender clemency?
My sole refuge, O Goddess, is your sacred law,
spoken timelessly by Shiva,
one teaching that manifests
    through all the scriptures of humanity,
unveiling our supreme identity.

This child cries out with melting heart:
"Ma Kali! Ma Kali! Ma Kali!
Only to merge with you
    do I desire to transcend death.
Permit me to draw my final breath
    right here and now
on the bank of the inward River Ganga,
standing on the breast of Shiva,
my entire being shining with your name."

Its value beyond assessment by the mind

Whom could I fear in the universe
    where my Mother is matriarch?
I live with perfect ease upon her estate,
indivisible awareness and bliss.
I am her direct tenant,
free from formality and hierarchy.

There is no payment of rent for this sanctuary,
this garden of nonduality,
its value beyond assessment by the mind.
Nor can my sacred abode be sold at auction,
for there are no owners and nothing to own.
The manager of Mother's holdings, Lord Shiva,
transcends every limited conception and transaction.
There is no disharmony or injustice here,
for there is no division, no separation.
Mother does not impose the heavy tax
    of religious obligation.
My only responsibility of stewardship
    is constant inward remembrance,
eternally breathing *Kali, Kali, Kali*.

This mad poet lover,
born directly from Divine Mother,
cherishes one consuming desire:
to purchase her diamond paradise of delight
    with the boundless treasure of pure love
and give it away freely to all beings.

Now please bring your small child home

My attraction to this world of convention
    consists of empty expectation
without the slightest ground.
I am a honey bee buzzing around
    the lotus flowers on a tapestry.
This enchanting scene, O Mahamaya,
is composed solely from your silken threads,
your brilliant strands of consciousness.

Playfully you persuaded me
    that the bitter fruit of egocentric desire
is sweeter than sugar.
Greedily, I consumed this strange fruit.
Its sharp taste remains in my mouth
    day after day.
You drew my soul to the relative plane
    by the promise of wonderful communion,
but this divine play in the mode of separation
    has been severely disappointing.

Sings your poet of mystic union:
"O Kali, the drama of my life
    was composed and acted out
in the blazing summer field of destiny.
Now please bring your small child home
    through the fragrant cool of evening,
cradled in your arms, lost in your gaze,
disappearing in your love."

I have a serious grievance to settle

I have a serious grievance to settle
   with the Mother of the Universe.
Even while apparently awake,
with you as my all-protecting Mother,
the house of mind and body
   is ransacked by robbers,
my countless egocentric impulses.
Every day I resolve to repeat your name
   as the most powerful defense,
but forget my good intention
   just as the intruders arrive.

I have caught on to the playfulness,
O Mother, by which you elude my willful grasp.
You bestow no power of inward prayer upon this child,
so you receive no consistent devotion from me.
I no longer regard this as my fault.
Only what you give me can I return to you
   as the sweet offering of divine remembrance.
Fame and infamy, good and bad tastes of life,
all phenomena are your graceful play.
Yet as you dance in ecstasy,
we are thrown into quandary.
O Goddess, lead us on your wisdom way!

This poet dares to sing her secret:
"Mother Mahamaya places a dream in every mind,
making it perceive the ashes of egocentricity
   as an abundance of cotton candy,
which it tastes with constant disappointment
   and shocked surprise.
Awaken now and be free!"

She is ever elusive, ever free

O miserable poet, be sensible for once!
Stop this constant crying
　　Mother, Mother, Mother.
Where do you imagine she could be?
Were this Divine Mother of yours a living goddess,
surely she would have come to you by now.
This madwoman whom you suppose to be
　　the all-victorious Warrior of Truth
must no longer be alive.

I will visit my stepmother, River Ganga.
At least her powerful presence
　　can be encountered by the five senses.
Beside the relentlessly flowing river of time,
I will place upon a flaming pyre
　　a Kali image made of sacred grass
and perform rites for her funeral.
I will observe the proscribed period of mourning
　　and then offer ceremonial rice
for her departed soul.

Awakening from this dark dream,
her poet cries with tears of contrition:
"O mind, why rebel against
　　Mother's wonderful inconceivability?
She is ever elusive, ever free.
Can you contain her, even momentarily?
Can you control Goddess activity?
Simply continue to intone *Ma! Ma! Ma!*
You will taste the honey of her mercy."

I have embraced you at last, Supreme Lady!

Ma Kali,
you transform compassionately
    into graceful Krishna,
surrounded by circles of ecstatic maidens,
lovers in the intimate embrace of timeless beauty.
Your manifestations are infinite, O Mother,
infinite the spiritual paths you generate.
Who can comprehend the fullness of your mystery?

Half your body assumes form as brilliant Radha,
most sublime adept on the path of love.
The other half appears as dark Krishna,
who is all-embracing love, free from duality.
You dance naked as fierce Goddess energy,
and then appear clad in Radha's charming sari.
As Kali, embodiment of freedom,
your black hair streams long and wild.
Then you appear with queenly tresses
    balanced on your head,
Krishna's flute of rapture
    resting in your dark blue hands.

O Kali! O inconceivability!
Your burning glance of ecstasy
    that drives Shiva mad with sheer abandon
now flows through the lovely eyes of Krishna.
The aspirants you awaken into profound longing
    are milkmaids in the pastures of purest passion.
The terrible thunder of Kali's laughter
    that causes heaven and earth to tremble
becomes a gentle cascade of melody
    to the tender ears of Krishna's lovers.

The beautiful black Warrior Goddess who strides across
    the sparkling universal ocean of blood
now splashes playfully as golden Radha
    in the crystal waters of River Jumna.

This poet laughs, lost in Mother's innate bliss,
her self-luminous transformation:
"Ma! Ma! Ma!
In the open space beyond meditation
    I glimpse your secret spontaneously.
Radha, Krishna, and Kali are one reality.
I have embraced you at last, Supreme Lady!"

O poet who constantly forgets

O poet who constantly forgets,
you have no idea how to keep accounts.
When you were born, you received
    the vast credit of timeless awareness,
but every moment since then you have plunged into debt.
If you could balance your spiritual resources
    with the expenses of temporality,
there would be no tension in your being.
You would be joyful and carefree.
But your expenditures from the capital of divine grace
    far exceed your sparse income
from personal efforts at deep concentration.
You alone are accountable for this imbalance,
which must be explained in full.

This helpless child of Mother
    exclaims in desperation:
"O mind, why such strange obsession
    to account for credits and for debits?
Just imbue your entire being
    with the one who is utterly unaccountable,
counting only *Kali, Kali, Kali.*"

Now only the Goddess remains

Primordial Mother of my essential being!
Single vessel in the sea of temporality!
Ma! Ma! Ma!
Only those cross-eyed with delusion
    imagine any separation
between Mother's play and Absolute Reality.
Kali's dancing energy and Shiva's pure tranquillity
    are simply one essence of awareness.

The Goddess transcends her own dance.
She is the womb of open space.
Glimpsing this, Shiva enters trance.
Yet Mother emerges into form and action
    in response to every prayer and longing.

Kali overflows with compassion
    for her lovers who are poor and simple,
overwhelming their astonished hearts
    with her most sublime adornments:
pure love and nondual wisdom.
This very universe becomes a radiant garden of bliss
    for those who repeat her name
with every heartbeat, every breath.

Each atom singing *Tara, Tara, Tara,*
entering Lord Shiva's brilliant death,
her human lover becomes the Absolute,
merged in bliss beneath her flashing feet.
Now only the Goddess remains.

This indolent poet can only weep:
"Those incapable of constant contemplation
    can hope to transcend

this hopeless maze of mere convention
   only through the grace of Mother Wisdom,
her liberating grace alone."

Everyone is babbling about what happens after death

Everyone is babbling about what happens after death.
Superstitious villagers insist we become
    peculiar wandering spirits,
while simple religious hearts assume our goal
    to be sweet heavenly existence.
Lovers long to play
    in eternal companionship with Divinity,
while mystics strive
    to merge completely with Divine Reality.
Scriptures of radical wisdom maintain
    that the apparent soul is like space within a jar.
When death shatters our earthen vessel,
only the open space of awareness remains.
Who is there to unify with whom?

This intoxicated poet who belongs to Goddess Kali
    knows all opinion to be void of substance.
Mother's mystery eludes
    every earnest practitioner or philosopher
who assumes negative or positive energy
    to be substantial or real.
This mirror mind and rainbow body
    are her marvelous play
through the transparent medium of her elements.
After death, her dancing elements flow on,
and simply Mother remains.

The singer of this liberating song
    laughs loud and long:
"We will be in the end
    what we were in the beginning,
clear bubbles forming and dissolving
    in the stream of timeless Mother Wisdom."

Do you not feel foolish adorning clay statues?

O mind, your delusion has not been removed
    by countless religious rites.
You have not apprehended the essence of Kali.
Look now! Can you see?
The realms of being that you separate habitually,
calling them heaven and earth, divinity and humanity,
are simply forms of one universal Mother.

You know the single truth, O mind,
with clarity and certainty.
Your very nature is this truth.
Why are you imagining constantly
    that you are ignorant?
Why create finite images and concepts
    of the living Goddess
who is infinite?
Mother's splendor manifests
    through every gem in the universe.
Do you not feel foolish adorning clay statues
    with wooden ornaments painted gold?
Mother feeds the boundless expanse of creatures
    from her own rich abundance.
Why present her rice and curry
    with such elaborate ceremony?
The Mother of the Universe treats with tenderness
    every manifest spark of her own infinite life.
What impels you to sacrifice to her
    the precious lives of goats and buffaloes?

With deep conviction, this poet cries:
"Only ecstatic love and selfless meditation
    can be offered to the Goddess of Wisdom.
External forms of worship and propitiation
    are bribes she will never accept."

I cannot live another moment

Falling under the spell of time,
I have wasted my time.
What awaits me, O Mother,
when this career on earth comes to an end?
Who will hear my cry
    when Death drags me by the hair?

I have learned from ancient scripture
    that Goddess Tara is the liberator
of those who travel through temporal existence.
Compassionate Tara, take responsibility for me!
Please purify the intentions of my heart
    so the cruel and clever enemy,
egocentric passion and compulsion,
can no longer laugh at me and deride me.

This poet has indulged a wandering mind
    lacking intelligence and strength.
I cannot live another moment
    without the hope of touching
with my forehead the wisdom feet of Kali,
blending with her completely,
assuming her identity.

This careless child turns to Mother only:
"A single glance from you
    will remove my fear forever."

Shiva is lost! Lost in Mother!

Hum with every breath Mother's powerful mantra,
Om Kali Ma, Om Kali Ma, Om Kali Ma.
These sacred sounds dissolve the fear of mortality
    that crystallizes in the subtle body,
diverting the current of conscious energy.
These very sounds transform Shiva,
the essence of divinity,
into an ecstatic wanderer,
abiding in cremation grounds
    where conventional earthly beauty
cannot veil Mother's infinite beauty,
the brilliant blackness of her open space.

Even in their deepest contemplation,
various exalted heavenly beings,
including Brahma, Lord of Creation,
have failed to penetrate her radiant mystery.
Shiva alone has abandoned his being
    beneath her dancing, red-soled feet,
merging with her entirely.
Spread the wonderful news everywhere:
Shiva is lost! Lost in Mother!
Even if you shout into his ears,
you will never disturb his conscious identity
    with all-embracing Mother Reality.

But this lazy poet
    remains absorbed only in obscurity:
"I stammer songs of nonduality,
yet lack the intense devotion for Goddess Kali
    that would empower me to taste and see."

My heart awakens to your truth

Mother of the Universe,
you reside deep within my secret heart.
Mysterious Kali, how can I say
    you are distant from me?
Yet you manifest so elusively,
O Goddess of cosmic illusion, O Mahamaya,
disguising your clear light with countless masks.
You assume contrasting roles
    to harmonize with every calling
of worship, prayer, and meditation,
but can you continue to elude the lover
    who knows that your surprising forms
express the single essence of awareness?

Ma! Ma! Ma!
I know you will not assume responsibility
    for willful travelers
who do not take refuge in you consciously.
Those content with the glass beads
    of self-centered existence
cannot discern the gold of self-surrender.

This singer of her spontaneous verses
    cries to the Wisdom Mother:
"O Goddess composed of consciousness,
my heart awakens to your truth
    like a flower naturally blossoming.
Please reveal your transparent presence
    within this lotus heart
as open space, forever shining."

The substance of every suffering will vanish

O wonderful Mahamaya,
who can analyze your dream power
    that projects the momentary universe?
O Goddess eternally mad with wisdom bliss,
why have you driven us mad instead
    with habitual diversion?

Lost within your magic projection,
we cannot recognize each other
    as strands of one consciousness.
Everyone lives in pallid imitation of everyone else,
seeking derivative experience
    instead of the original way.
This is the ironic twist in Ma Kali's play,
the only real agony caused by her strange theater:
our inability to see her as she is,
to be her as we are.

Yet this poet of Mother Wisdom
    is empowered to proclaim sweet solace:
"The substance of every suffering will vanish
    through her boundless grace."

A country fair for those mad with love

Drive me out of my mind, O Mother!
What use is esoteric knowledge
    or philosophical discrimination?
Transport me totally with the burning wine
    of your all-embracing love.
Mother of Mystery, who imbues with mystery
    the hearts of those who love you,
immerse me irretrievably
    in the stormy ocean without boundary,
pure love, pure love, pure love.

Wherever your lovers reside
    appears like a madhouse
to common pereption.
Some are laughing with your freedom,
others weep tears of your tenderness,
still others dance, whirling with your bliss.
Even your devoted Gautama, Moses,
Krishna, Jesus, Nanak, and Muhammad
    are lost in the rapture of pure love.

This poet stammers,
overcome with longing:
"When? When? When?
When will I be granted companionship
    with her intense lovers?"
Their holy company is heavenly,
a country fair for those mad with love,
where every distinction
    between master and disciple
disappears.

This lover of love sings:
"Mother! Mother! Mother!

Who can fathom your mystery,
your eternal play of love with love?
You are divine madness, O Goddess,
your love the brilliant crown of madness.
Please make this poor poet madly wealthy
    with the infinite treasure of your love."

I ponder my dilemma ceaselessly

None of my profound longing
    has come to fruition.
My mind is full of anguish
    I have held secretly within me.
Looking back over this life, I can clearly see
    the pervasive misery of relative existence.
What hope can persist
    for future happiness?

Most compassionate Mother,
six enemies, ego and senses,
have kept constant company with me,
never allowing me to think or act selflessly,
always drawing me into duality.

This singer of painful truth cries:
"Kali! Kali! Kali!
I ponder my dilemma ceaselessly,
finding no resolution.
I can only conclude that taking refuge
    at your lotus feet of purifying fire
has somehow caused me to suffer
    so intensely and so consciously."

Only you

O sublime Kali,
you dance in solitude as naked truth.
Your black hair streams wildly
    as pure freedom.
You alone can fulfill with your very being
    my soul's most secret yearning.
No one else can offer any real response
    to this transcendent desire for union
burning constantly in my heart.

O Mother, please tell me whether
    your illumination will ever
sweep away this separate self.
You must! You must!
To you alone with every breath
    I confess the ultimate realization
for which I thirst.

Ma! Ma! Ma!
No being within countless heavenly realms
    or across this vast earth
can truly understand my desperate longing.
Only you.

My Divine Mother plays the role of a poor village woman

Mother of the Universe,
I have a serious quarrel with you.
You have overwhelmed me
    with responsibility for family,
yet fail to provide the minimal prosperity
    that can keep family life in harmony.
Ma Kali! Ma Kali! Ma Kali!
Even you quarrel with your consort
    because he lives as a wandering sage,
providing you absolutely no support!

The transcendent knowing
    that is Shiva's very being
demonstrates for seekers
    the most powerful mode of contemplation.
But such formless meditation
    is much too demanding
for this child who can only cry Mother's name.

The practice of selfless giving
    is superior to religious ritual,
but for this noble path, service to humanity,
certain basic assets are necessary.
Remember, Mother, even Radha,
lover of divine love incarnate,
bears gifts when visiting her beloved Krishna,
her priceless blue jewel of ecstasy.
What have you provided me
    to bring you as an offering?

Dissolving every sense of expectation,
my Divine Mother plays the role
    of a poor village woman,
barefoot, covered with ashes.

But no longer can you conceal
      your inconceivable wealth,
O mysterious Black Queen.
I clearly see the treasurer of the heavenly realm
      standing humbly beside you as your servant.

Hour after hour,
this awakened poet sings:
"Jai Ma Kali! Victory to Kali!
To you alone, my blissful Mother,
belongs universal victory!"

All rituals of religion have fallen away

My entire life has now become the Goddess,
immersed in her own secret contemplation.

I received this all-embracing Mother way
    from an adept of the open space
beyond meditation,
one who dwells in a brilliant landscape
    where there is neither night nor day.

I cannot practice formal concentration
    at the sacred hours of dawn and twilight,
because the sun of her wisdom never rises or sets.
All my hours have become her midnight.
My once fertile dream-fields
    are now completely barren of fruit,
because dream and dreamless sleep
    have disappeared into Mother.
I feel I have been awake and clear
    for countless eons.

Returning the veils of conventional sleep
    and conventional waking
to the cosmic ignorance from which they spring,
I sing the lullaby of Mother Wisdom,
so sleeping and waking fall asleep forever.

Mother's fire has purified all dross
    from the gold of consciousness.
My only desire is to shape your human temple
    from this golden energy,
O blissful Goddess,
adorning it with your priceless gems:
compassion, beauty, clarity, intensity.

How I long to behold this sanctuary,
this fully awakened humanity,
diamond refuge for all suffering beings!

The singer of this hymn of enlightenment
    now cries aloud in ecstasy:
"On my forehead I bear
    the treasure of incomparability,
the crest-jewel of illumination,
the radiance of pure love alone.
I have known her final secret.
One with Absolute Reality
    is Mother's dynamic play.
All rituals of religion have fallen away."

How courageous I must be!

O majestic Kali! O living mystery!
You who sweep away every difficulty!
Why do you refuse to intervene
    for this poet plunged in poverty?

Sublime Goddess, why do you avoid
    every display of wealth and power?
Why do you prefer cremation grounds
    to your transparent palace of jewels?
You resemble your own consort, the Renunciate,
who lives only on the crushed hemp leaves
    of transcendent knowing.

Whoever loves you, Ma Tara,
shines with inward illumination.
The secret lives of your humble lovers
    far surpass in wonderful intensity
the naked limbs and matted hair
    of the outwardly ascetic way.
The subtle bodies of these pure lovers
    are adorned invisibly
by the beauty of inward renunciation,
the realization of nonduality.

Great Mother Goddess,
through your inconceivable will alone
    my soul incarnates upon this earth.
I no longer find compelling reason or motivation.
You present me experience after experience
    filled with ambiguity and misery
and still I repeat your august name,
Kali, Kali, Kali.
How courageous I must be!

Everyone is whispering
    that the destitute poet now singing
falsely claims to be the child of a wealthy mother.
But who can begin to understand, O blissful Kali,
our most secret intimacy,
and the rich meaning of the poverty
    you generously present to me?

What can you do but cry aloud Ma, Ma, Ma *and be free?*

Consider the foolishness of the game
    you are playing, O mind,
and become ashamed.
O noble black bee, you should taste only
    the pure nectar of awareness,
attracted by the intense fragrance of Ma Kali,
whose wisdom feet are vast lotuses
    streaming with perfume.
How can you continue to drink the poison
    of egocentric gratification?

O essential mind,
you are infinitely more refined
    than organs of action and perception.
In the kingdom of consciousness,
you are natural sovereign.
Yet you accept as constant companions
    the most limited and negative intentions.
What minor potentate have you become?
Bloated by arrogance, by flattery inflated,
your royal gracefulness is dissipated.
Only when the body lies trampled
    beneath Death's senseless feet
will you realize your basic error:
turning away from your own natural purity.

Seasons of childhood, youth, and maturity
    pass with deceptive slowness, O mind.
Unaware, you suffer the anguish of self-obsession,
like a solitary prisoner in a narrow cell.
Those who live in selfless ecstasy
    are released from confinement instantly,
entering the open space of nonduality,
compassionate warriors on earth,

joyfully and courageously serving
    the Warrior Goddess of unitive wisdom.

Laughing aloud,
this liberated poet now asks everyone:
"When you grow fatally sick or old,
when Death draws near to strike its blow,
terrible yet illusory,
what can you do but cry aloud
    Ma, Ma, Ma
and be free?"

Why is Mother Kali so radiantly black?

Why is Mother Kali so radiantly black?
Because she is so powerful,
even mentioning her name destroys delusion.
Because she is so beautiful,
Lord Shiva, Conqueror of Death,
lies blissfully vanquished
    beneath her red-soled feet.

There are subtle hues of blackness,
but her bright complexion
    is the mystery that is utterly black,
overwhelmingly black, wonderfully black.
When she awakens in the lotus shrine
    within the heart's secret cave,
her blackness becomes the mystic illumination
    that causes the twelve-petal blossom there
to glow more intensely than golden embers.

Her lovely form is the incomparable Kali-black,
blacker than the King of Death.
Whoever gazes upon this radiant blackness
    falls eternally in love
and feels no attraction to any other,
discovering everywhere only her.

This poet sighs deeply:
"Where is this brilliant Lady,
this Black Light beyond luminosity?
Though I have never seen her,
simply hearing her name,
the mind becomes absorbed completely
    in her astonishing reality.
Om Kali! Om Kali! Om Kali!"

My Kali flies millions of mind kites

My Kali flies millions of mind kites
    in the windy bazaar of relativity,
human egos that dart and float
    in the empty sky,
secured only by invisible strings,
Mother's power of miraculous activity.

Kali constructs these marvelous kites
    from cosmic elements
to express her own sublime joy.
Their wood, glue, and paper bodies
    are composed of bone, nerve, and skin.
The colorful pattern of each kite is unique,
its design intricate and refined.

The kite strings are soaked in sticky resin,
egocentric pleasure, to make them hold strong,
and these strings are imbued with ground glass,
Mother's liberating wisdom,
to make them sharp.
When one kite in a hundred thousand is cut free
    by the razor edge of nonduality,
you laugh in delight, O Goddess,
and clap your hands with childlike glee,
sounding your high-pitched cry of victory.

This poet is thrown into ecstasy:
"May the kite of my mind break free,
ride the great wind of divine energy
    across the ocean of opacity,
and drift down gently
    on the transparent shore
of Kali's mystery."

I have turned away from Mother's shadow play

O Goddess of revolutionary wisdom,
your terrible garland of freshly severed heads
    inspires complete renunciation
of birth and death, concept and convention,
this cosmic drama you demonstrate clearly
    to be your own magical display.

You have taught me to address reality
    with your most tender name, O Mother,
awakening the divine madness of love,
so I am constantly weeping *Ma, Ma, Ma.*
Where did you discover a name so sweet,
replete with the nectar of timeless awareness?
Citizens of the mundane realm call this lover
    the crazy poet of the Cosmic Mother.
Even members of my own family deride me.
But would I stray from your way
    because of any opinion, beloved Kali?

Limited minds may form whatever judgment they please.
I will continue to sing *Kali, Kali, Kali.*
Conventional honor and dishonor are equal to me.
I have turned away from Mother's shadow play
    and made her dancing, red-soled feet,
her dynamic wisdom essence,
the meaning and goal of my existence.

Merged in her gaze of nonduality,
I no longer even hear
    misguiding chatter from the world.

Watch Kali swing! Let her swing!

Face beaming with awesome splendor,
the bright black Goddess
    rocks blissfully on the red lotus
of my secret heart.
The great wind of rising awareness
    swings her gently,
night and day.

Though she manifests luminous channels of energy
    that travel throughout the precious human body,
my dynamic Mother is none other
    than the vast peace of Absolute Reality.
Her dark blue feet of mystery reveal crimson soles
    flashing brilliantly as she swings,
like lightning emerging from black clouds,
filling my body with subtle ecstasy.
One glance at her inconceivable beauty
    dissolves egocentric passion and delusion
forever.

The awakened lover who attains the vision
    of Mother's mystic lotus swing
leaves her lap and develops to maturity.
Again and again, this inebriated poet sings:
"Watch Kali swing! Let her swing!"

Cremation grounds are your great delight

Mysterious Ma Kali,
cremation grounds are your great delight,
for there you release souls from mundane experience.
I have transformed my heart into a cremation ground
    so you will be attracted here to dance
as flames of liberating bliss.

O Wisdom Goddess,
my limited desire has been consumed
    on the blazing pyre of renunciation.
O Goddess of Freedom,
I am surrounded by the ashes
    that were my assumptions,
waiting ardently for you to come.

Please manifest in the brilliant midnight hour
    of this renouncing heart.
Please dance to the intense drum of my longing
    upon the breast of Absolute Reality
that appears as Shiva, Conqueror of Death,
breathless beneath your flashing feet.

The singer of this strange song is waiting,
eyes wide open in the wakefulness
    beyond meditation.

How well I know that fool's sorry fate!

Mother of the Universe,
please grant me conscious refuge at your feet.
You who redeem with a single glance!
You who dissolve the fear of death!
Goddess Tara, your subtle form
    is the transcendent sound *Om! Om! Om!*
Consort of the Absolute! Displayer of the Absolute!
Fountain of Illumination!
You are the single power that streams
    as divine beauty
into the ocean of inconceivability,
the open space of nonduality.

You are physical universes
    and nonphysical dimensions of luminosity,
both root cause of every being
    and original source, untouched by causality.
Your living energy, O Goddess,
abides within the primal lotus of awareness,
foundation of the precious human body.
You are Mother Reality,
beyond every description
    by religion or esoteric wisdom.

You manifest as transparent consciousness
    and as the principle of tangibility.
Your life alone, Great Mother,
is the breath of every creature.
You emanate, sustain, and absorb
    innumerable planets, planes, and spheres.
Your name of liberation,
Kali, Kali, Kali,
is the nectar of timeless awareness,
the sweet honey of essentiality.

The fool who ignores your pervasive reality
    suffers in soul, mind, and body,
drowning in the poisoned well of egocentricity.
Again and again, this poet laments:
"How well I know that fool's sorry fate!"

See all in her and her as all

The Mother of the Universe
    captivates every world with her beauty.
Her long hair streams as waves of cosmic energy.
This drunken poet has fallen forever in love
    with her glorious black luminosity.
Mystic union with her transcendent blackness
    is experienced by intense lovers.
This blackness even exhilarates Shiva,
supreme Knower of Reality,
and inspires as well every heavenly being,
every ardent saint, every awakened sage.

Lord Shiva, essence of divinity,
meditates on her black form ceaselessly
    as she dances in his heart.
Her beautiful blackness flows
    as the graceful play of Krishna,
who removes all notions of mundane existence
    from ecstatic milkmaids,
souls filled with sweet devotion.
Then Lord Krishna, garlanded with wildflowers,
transforms once more into original Kali,
wielding her sword of wisdom
    that cuts away the veil of multiplicity.

The Black Goddess and her companions
    are eternally sixteen, timelessly dancing.
How my mysterious Mother shines,
full moon of Goddess Wisdom that never wanes,
surrounded by these piercing stars,
her revolutionary spiritual children!

Utterly lost in delight, her poet lover sings:
"This is the dawning of enlightenment,
the awakening to nonduality.
Her form and every form are now blending
    into one radiant blackness.
O mind, despise no being, reject no path.
See all in her and her as all."

Her nature as pure reality can never be described!

O foolish mind, do not indulge in hatred
    for any sacred way
if you wish to enter pure reality.

With desperate longing for truth alone,
the singer of this song has plunged
    into the ocean of ancient scriptures,
discovering at last that my blissful Mother,
her black hair falling free in ecstasy,
is the living power within every religious symbol,
the coherent core of every philosophy.

She is the warrior spirit, Kali dancing,
and she is Shiva, all-transcending.
She is ineffable sweetness, Radha-Krishna,
the love play that dissolves conventionality.
She is Sita-Ram, compassionately wise,
the complete evolution of humanity.

O Mother Divine, your power alone
    manifests as Shiva the Sublime,
sounding his ram's horn in mountain solitude,
and as Krishna smiling tenderly,
surrounded by ecstatic lovers,
playing bamboo flute in the fertile river valley.
Mother! Mother! Mother!
Your secret power shines as Lord Rama,
bearing the bow of justice,
and as Great Goddess Kali,
wielding the sword of nonduality.

Removing these veils, O Goddess,
you dance naked as timeless awareness
    on the body of your consort,

who lies still, enraptured, also naked truth,
merged in union with the Absolute.

O Mother Power!
You abide in the dusty cremation ground
    as world-liberating Kali.
You reside within the noble palace of leadership.
You dance through the fragrant green landscape of love.

The Mother of the Universe
    is both woman and man
when they meet in blissful embrace,
dedicating their union to conscious oneness.
Mother alone manifests as loyal brother
    and as consecrated wife
along the sacred way of selfless daily life.

This poet is struck with amazement and cries:
"Her nature as pure reality can never be described!
She is fullness! She is completeness!
My Mother dwells in all beings
    as their secret essence.
At her wisdom feet I find every fragrance,
every scripture, every place of pilgrimage."

I would not even care to be an emperor

Mother of the Universe,
I have no desire to exercise power.
I would not even care to be an emperor.
Sweet Mother, please grant me
    two simple meals each day
and wealth enough to thatch the palm roof
    of my clean earthen house,
where I offer dreaming and waking
    as red flowers at your feet.

My green village dwelling is the abode
    of your golden radiance, O Goddess.
What need have I for more elaborate construction?
If you surround me with the complex architecture
    of stature and possession,
I will refuse to call you *Mother* ever again.

O Kali, give me just enough to serve lovingly
    whatever guests may visit me.
Plain metal plates and cups will do.
Daily existence in the heart of my extended family
    is the worship beyond worship
that perceives Mother Reality
    as every being, every situation, every breath.

I will never leave this natural way of life
    to become a stern ascetic
or a teacher honored by the world.
There is only one longing this poet's soul
    declares over and over:
"Mother! Mother! Mother!
May every moment of my existence
    merge completely with your essence."

What is the meaning of your nakedness?

O sublime Goddess! O naked oneness!
What is the meaning of your nakedness?
Are you shameless, Divine Lady?
Yet even when discarding
    royal silks and golden ornaments
for earrings, bracelets, and anklets
    fashioned from human bone,
you retain the dignity of bearing
    suited to the daughter of a king.

What wild customs you follow, Ma Kali,
trampling on the chest of your noble husband.
You are the naked intensity of divine creativity,
your consort naked transcendence.
Together you roam cremation grounds
    as mystic union of space and energy,
liberating the soul from its self-imposed destiny.

O Mother of the Universe,
this child is terrified by your naked truth,
your unthinkable blackness, your sheer infinity.
Please cover your reality with a gentle veil.
Why have you thrown away the necklace of pearls
    that enhances your divine beauty,
wearing instead this awesome garland of heads,
freshly severed by the sword of nonduality?

The singer of this gnostic hymn is struck dumb
    and is barely able to cry:
"Ma, Ma, Ma!
So powerful is your lovely ferocity
    that even your dancing consort Shiva,
ground and essence of divinity,
has fainted with awe,
dissolved in transparency."

Encircle the wild elephant of mundane mind

Encircle the wild elephant of mundane mind
    with the magical sapphire tether.
Contemplate Kali's midnight-blue feet forever!
Sever the limits you create
    by every habitual thought and action,
wielding her sword of wisdom energy,
Kali, Kali, Kali.

O acquisitive mind,
ceaselessly you accumulate egocentric pleasure.
You carry this heavy basket on your head everywhere,
barely noticing its fragrance of fish and rotting fruit.
Your consciousness also bears the crushing weight
    of earth, air, fire, water,
and labors under these burdens day and night.
Without acknowledging it,
the heart is being ravaged continuously
    by all-pervasive suffering.
This terrible experience is granted by Kali,
whose potent blackness is a great storm cloud
    that releases the healing rain of compassion.

O foolish poet,
moment by moment, your life span is diminishing.
Desperately making pilgrimage to holy places
    merely wears out the body.
You will receive Mother's breath of wisdom
    while sitting at home in quiet contemplation,
disciplined by the responsibility of daily life.

The singer of this song has reached
    the final boundary:
"O Mother, I have no idea how to attain
    liberation from egocentricity.

Ceremonial worship is only theater,
study of scripture mere mental exercise.
Your living name alone can burst my being
    and set me free."

Your life is the life of the entire universe

O my dreaming mind,
awaken now and remain awake forever!
Sleeping with eyes open as you walk through the world
    is the strange sleep of delusion.
How long will you remain deceived
    by egocentric projects and projection,
your original awareness veiled
    by vivid dreams, imagined to be real?

This routine life of empty repetition,
this constant drive for gratification,
wastes your spiritual power, O mind.
You are dreaming!
You dream away your existence!
These waking dreams are fueled by selfish craving.
Replace the darkness of this deluded sleep
    with repose that is peaceful and genuine,
selfless concentration on Kali's feet of wisdom.
This is the radiant treasure you truly desire.

The essence of your being will awaken
    through this devoted meditation.
You will be enlightened by Goddess light,
union of ecstatic love and transcendent insight.

Speaking with Mother's own voice,
this poet calls:
"O essential mind,
your life is the life of the entire universe.
Awaken into perpetual contemplation.
Every dream veil will dissolve."

Will you ever heed my mad longing?

O Wisdom Goddess,
how long will you keep me in poverty?
When will you exalt my destiny, O tender Mother,
who is always compassionate to the poor?
You know I am impoverished.
My ceremonial worship is destitute,
and I am bereft of simple prayer.
I can only sit and stare
    into your boundless space.
Will you ever heed my mad longing
    to merge completely into you?

Great Goddess, Liberator of the Universe,
will you ever replace my conventional identity
    with your feet of mystery,
your inconceivability?
You alone are omniscient.
What sort of child I am,
you know through and through.
But when does a mother ever discard her child,
however thoughtless or rebellious it may be?
Who else can understand my existence, O Mother?
Who else can express infinite mercy?

This poet overflows with ecstasy:
"I can only sing the beautiful seed sounds
    Ma Kali, Ma Kali.
Her very nature is to liberate all beings,
awakening them beyond ultimacy.
Even Shiva,
greatest adept of transcendent insight,
is chanting her name fervently,
desiring only her sweet intimacy.

O small self, you are a sparkling fish

O small self, you are a sparkling fish
    at play in the ocean of consciousness,
and your life is swiftly coming to its end.
Death will skim above you and throw its sharp net.
You will not be protected by your watery world,
for selfish actions have kept you in the shallows.

The fisherman's fatal net will surround you suddenly.
Why do you remain so near the surface of relative existence
    where Death is granted its fishing grounds?
Yet there is still time.
Leave the dangerous shoreline, mundane mind,
and plunge into silent profundity,
the black waters of Mother Kali's mystery.

What do they care for the opinion of the world?

The most exalted experience of bliss
    in any realm of being
is directly knowing the universal Mother,
the supremely blissful one.
Ecstatic lovers of Kali the Sublime
    are not pilgrims to sacred shrines,
for they hear all existence
    singing the glory of the Goddess.

These lovers of living truth
    follow no schedule of worship or meditation.
They have lost their limited wills
    in the limitless will of Mother,
perceiving her alone as acting through all action.

Those who have made Kali's feet of infinite delight
    the goal and meaning of their life
spontaneously forget every craving
    for egocentric power and pleasure.
These beings of pure love sail effortlessly
    across the heavy seas of birth and death,
for they are in constant contact only
    with the root and essence of reality.

Mother's poet sings in rapture:
"What do they care for the opinion of the world?
These lovers, eyes half-closed with inward gaze,
are drinking night and day
    the sweet and powerful nectar,
Mother! Mother! Mother!"

No limited vessel can cross a shoreless sea

This beginningless ocean of beings
    who are born and who are dying
is without shores.
No limited vessel can cross a shoreless sea.
The power that flows from Mother's feet
    is my only hope on this tremendous journey,
my only vehicle, my only provision,
my only certainty.

O Tara who bears beings tenderly
    across the dangerous waters of relativity,
please carry me through this constant misery,
both obvious and subtle,
this relentless ocean of life-and-death struggle,
this turmoil of gigantic waves.
The poet now singing trembles in every nerve
    at the terrible vision of universal suffering,
and fears death by drowning
    in the stormy expanse of creation and destruction.

Goddess Tara! Goddess Tara!
Permeate me with your own enlightenment!
Make me your humble servant, your intimate attendant.
Sail me across this boundless sea
    in the vessel of devotion to your reality.
The vast tempest of relativity never abates.
My limbs are quaking
    as I ceaselessly call your name.
You must respond to my longing.
You must!

Om Tara, Om Tara, Om Tara.
Your name alone is the living essence
    of this appearance called relative existence.

I sink into the sea of time
    only when I forget your name.

Her poet laments and prays:
"I am wasting this sacred human life.
Please sever whatever binds me
    to individuality and temporality.
To whom can I possibly
    entrust my soul but you,
my spiritual Mother?"

Can the thorny scrub tree bear sweet fruit?

My precious sisters and brothers,
what use is this marvelous human body
    if it does not dance in holy ecstasy?
Impure the tongue that fails to transform
    every utterance into *Kali, Kali, Kali.*
Blind the eyes that do not perceive every creature
    as blissful expression of the Cosmic Mother.
Ignorant and dangerous the mind
    that cannot absorb every thought
in the beauty of Kali's lotus feet.

May these ears be struck by lightning!
What purpose can they truly serve
    if every sound is not clearly heard
as the sweet nectar of her liberating name.
How can we honor these hands
    that gather daily sustenance
unless their function is understood
    as offering red flowers to the black Goddess?
What value have these feet,
treading the earth day and night,
unless they carry us with humility and joy
    to her sacred shrines,
to hearts where she is awake?

Can the Mother of the Universe be embraced
    unless every organ of action and perception
becomes oriented toward her?
This poet can only laugh at the vanity
    of mundane expectation,
asking everyone:
"Can the thorny scrub tree bear sweet fruit?"

Kali's wisdom thunder rumbles

Radiant black storm clouds
    expand across the sky of pure awareness.
The peacock of my mind reveals its brilliant colors,
dancing in the bliss of holy expectation.
Kali's wisdom thunder rumbles
    with her power that can level mountains.
The fiery tracery of lightning flashes
    forms her wonderful smile of ecstasy.

The lover of Ma Kali gazes intently,
tears pouring down like monsoon rain.
Only these most precious drops
    can quench the thirst of the heart,
that rare winging creature
    who drinks only from limitless sky,
never from limited pools or streams.
To be born in this body composed of common clay
    is a heavy burden for the soaring soul.
To incarnate again and again
    across this vast planetary realm
can never slake our burning thirst for reality.

Proclaims the liberated one
    who sings this gnostic hymn:
"No more birth from the womb of matter,
only emanation from Divine Mother."

Those who long for conscious union with reality

Who is this astonishing feminine presence
    dancing in the universal field of battle?
Truly naked, eternally sixteen,
with magnificent dignity she stands
    on the breast of Absolute Reality
that assumes the aspect of snow-white Shiva,
his body also naked truth
    as he sleeps in supernal contemplation.

All blood ever shed in sacrifice or conflict
    streams down her brilliant black limbs
like crimson blossoms floating on dark waters.
Her face is diamond bright, clearer than the full moon.
Infinite wisdom energy pulsates
    through her mysterious blackness.
Her powerful wisdom laughter
    awakens and heals,
flowing in wave after wave of sweet nectar.

This poet is overwhelmed,
singing with tears of rapture:
"Those who long for conscious union with reality
    should meditate with constancy
on the dark blue lotus feet of Kali,
enshrined in the secret heart of humanity,
ensuring the liberation of all finite beings
    from the illusion of finitude."

Kali's sword and Krishna's flute are one

O partially perceiving mind,
your basic error of double vision
    has not been corrected.
Though profoundly attracted to worship
    Divine Reality as feminine,
its masculine aspect remains foreign to you.
Why are you unable to perceive the embracing unity
    behind every manifestation of divinity?

O divided mind,
your narrow devotion to the Goddess
    is mere self-seeking and self-adoration.
You have not yet entered the radical contemplation
    where she reveals her final secret:
Kali's sword and Krishna's flute are one.
Nor have you encountered the union of Shiva and Krishna,
the confluence of two great rivers:
transcendent knowledge and incarnate love.

This poet sings only plain truth:
"Still confused by multiplicity,
your eloquent prayers remain hypocrisy.
You still distinguish sharply
    between Shiva, Krishna, and Kali.
O deluded mind,
with eyes wide open and functioning,
you remain totally blind."

Now put down your terrible sword

O Mother of the Universe,
to you I submit my being
    in constant prostration.
Why do you refuse to grant me even one glance?
O Goddess, you are engaged
    in the ecstatic play of manifestation
and immersed as well in the contemplation
    of transcendent unity.
Is this why you do not turn toward me?

What incomprehensible drama
    are you unfolding on the planetary plane
and in the subtle realms of heaven and hell?
Anyone who glimpses a small fraction
    of your all-encompassing reality
longs to taste nonduality,
exclaiming spontaneously *Ma, Ma, Ma,*
weeping with astonishment and abandon.

O Mother,
your power alone projects and dissolves
    the rainbow of the cosmos.
Transcendent knowledge, taking Shiva's form,
faints beneath the blissful touch of your dancing feet.
Your thunderous laughter is terrifying
    to those proclaiming boundary or division.
Your graceful limbs stream with sacrificial blood
    being shed throughout the universe.

O Tara, original radiance,
you are the conscious light alive within all creatures.
O fierce Mother protectress of souls,
grant your nondual wisdom as my sole refuge.
Take me into your annihilating arms of love.

Mother, Mother, Mother!
Please manifest your gentle aspect
    as Goddess Saraswati, smiling delicately,
clad in the rainbow silk of tranquillity,
bearing her brilliant musical instrument,
improvising in the mode of mercy.

Kali is the new-moon night of mystery,
Saraswati the dawn of harmony.
O Goddess, this child has contemplated
    your awesome midnight so intensely.
Now put down your terrible sword.
Bathe me in the rising sun,
your healing rays of music and sweet wisdom.

You have not yet encountered the brilliant Magician

O mind, awaken to your innate purity
    and be perfectly at rest.
Cease to wander about, endlessly searching.
You must not travel in any direction,
not even the slightest distance.
You will receive the treasure of illumination
    at the very heart and ground of your being.

Pure mind is supreme spiritual wealth,
the alchemical principle that transforms
    all it touches into golden radiance.
Pure mind is the diamond with infinite facets
    that fulfills every aspiration,
constantly generating a profusion of other gems:
knowledge, love, beauty, compassion.

Pilgrimage to various temples and shrines
    creates fatigue and diversion.
Do not become obsessed with seeking.
Bathe at the sacred confluence of great rivers
    found deep within the human body
where three subtle nerve channels meet.
Breathe the sanctified atmosphere
    of the most remote, peaceful retreat,
the lotus wilderness of primal awareness.

This poet sings with adamantine conviction:
"The world of nature and culture
    is an intricate magical display.
You have not yet encountered the brilliant Magician.
She resides within each breath, each thought,
each movement, each perception."

O blissful Mother, you alone remain

Mother, what need is there to lead me
   through further trial and suffering?
Ma Kali, you are the warrior of truth,
so you must listen to what is true.
The final test to which you can submit me
   is to take my life-breath,
but I feel no confinement within existence,
no apprehension about death.

Living and dying are the same to me.
This body will dissolve inevitably.
What reason have I to brood over destiny
   when my mind is constantly immersed
in contemplation of your reality?
O you who melt even transcendent knowledge!
Ma! Ma! Ma!
The more you intensify the waves of relativity,
the more sport I will enjoy.

The crew on this vessel of mind and body,
organs of action, perception, and intellection,
are disciplined by concentration
   on your lotus feet, Great Goddess.
Do you think they will become frightened
   and allow the boat to sink
in the vast storm of your manifestation?
And were my ship to go down suddenly
   in the ocean of temporality,
I would dive with delight into the deeps
   and drink the water of death fearlessly,
for my essence has already plunged
   into your essence.

With every breath I am dying joyfully,
reflecting without cessation
    on the body's dissolution.
What further teaching has the world to give me?
I continue to appear simply
    as an empty wooden frame in human form,
moved about and held together
    by Mother's inscrutable power.

This mad poet sings:
"When the conventional frame of ego disappears,
O blissful Mother, you alone remain.
You alone can discern
    who you are and who I am.
Is there any distinction?"

You will never comprehend my Mother

Is Kali merely Shiva's playful consort?
Although he is pure death-dissolving knowledge,
Shiva prostrates his entire being before the Goddess.

She flows upward through six lotus centers
    within the subtle body,
guiding the mystical ascension of humanity.
Mother Kali is also inclusive reality,
encountered as an infinite lotus sea
    at the culmination of the human journey.
She is the beautiful black Warrior Goddess
    whose dynamic truth force
destroys countless forms of the ego-enemy.

O limited mind,
can you interpret her wild activity?
What conventional queen would dance fiercely
    on the breast of a king
who is Absolute Reality?

This poet is enlightened and proclaims:
"Goddess play is inconceivability.
O sisters and brothers, struggle to fathom her
    with every fiber of mental energy.
Your intelligence will be purified,
but you will never comprehend my Mother."

Are you a Goddess made of stone?

The torrent of time will continue to flow.
Somehow my days of anguish will pass.
Only the saga of your relentless testing of this soul
	will remain, O Mother of the Universe.
The brilliance of the name, *Ma Tara,*
will be forever tarnished by the atrocious suffering
	of this child who calls only to you!

I came to the world bazaar at your invitation.
After browsing through the wares of relativity,
finding only ambiguity and diversion,
I am waiting for a boat to take me home.
O Mother, the sun of my life is about to set,
chill and darkness are approaching.
I now perceive the mystic vessel that returns to you.
The boatman fills its hold with the precious treasure
	of those whose prayer has been pure,
but threatens to leave this destitute poet behind.

O Mother, the stern helmsman is demanding my fare.
Where will I obtain the spiritual wealth to pay?
The singer of this lament cries out in desperation:
"Are you a Goddess made of stone?
Cast one benign glance
	to cover the expense of my passage,
or I will dive into the ocean of temporality
	and swim across the raging midnight sea,
lost in contemplation of your secret glory,
chanting *Kali, Kali, Kali.*"

How can you hope to grasp her dancing feet?

O blissful Kali,
accept my congratulations.
You have enthralled the universe entirely
    with your countless transformations.
Your ultimate magic feat is to throw every being
    a sacred black stone, your very essence,
so that realization of mystic identity
    will be its final destiny.

You are so adept in magic, Ma Kali,
that you even draw the Father God,
who is all-transcending knowledge,
into your sweet madness,
your play of indivisible love.
As timeless awareness, you remain uninvolved,
producing the magic theater, divine creativity,
from the interplay of inertia, balance, and activity.
This avid worshiper of Mother is shocked
    that even supremely wise Lord Shiva
cannot realize Kali's true nature.

O supremely foolish poet,
how can you hope to grasp her dancing feet
    that elude even Shiva's comprehension?
She has clearly driven you mad as well
    with the magic of her love.

I know and I know that I know

Ma! Ma! Ma!
Why are you attempting to hide from my gaze?
I have realized at last the true nature
    of prayer and meditation.
They are simply your own play
    as longing and as aspiration.

You may try to veil your presence
    by allowing good fortune to pour into the lives
of all except those who devotedly worship you,
but I can now evoke your sparkling energy
    at the very root of this body.
You are no longer able to conceal yourself
    or appear distant from me.
My very breath and being
    bond with your potent mystery,
and I experience your power alone
    as my own inviolate strength.

I know and I know that I know.
Liberation from the strange illusion of not knowing
    has been attained only through you.
What more is there for you to give me
    or withhold from me?
No one can remove this realization.
Not even you.

I have bound the Goddess at the center of my being
    with strands of diamond knowing.
This courageous poet is now waiting.
Can the Mother of the Universe
    unravel my knots of pure love?

August Kali is the destroyer of every limit

Mind and senses caught by her play,
I attempt to shape an image of inconceivability
    from common thought and common clay.
But is the Mother of the Universe born from earth?
My creative labors are misdirected.
I am lost in her illusion of perspective.

The Goddess holds high her sword of wisdom light
    and wears as a garland of severed heads
the false ideas of separate identity she mercifully cuts away.
Can this living Goddess, composed of pure consciousness,
be represented by metal, stone, or clay?
Can any inanimate image
    heal and illuminate mind and body
as Kali does for those who turn toward her reality?
This poet has heard from the lips of awakened sages
    that Mother's resplendent blackness
lights and enlightens the entire universe.
Can the vision of such a brilliant countenance
    be produced by black dye on mud and straw?

The Goddess has three eyes:
sun of knowledge, moon of love,
and fire of cosmic dissolution.
What artist can create such a gaze?
August Kali is the destroyer of every limit.
How can limited representation contain her?
Only she can wash the stains of conventional concepts
    from the bright cloth of primal awareness,
revealing her indescribable nature
    to the child who sings this song.

O foolish mind, time is running away

O tongue, please shape constantly
    the sacred sound *Kali, Kali, Kali.*
O mind, be ceaselessly aware!
The Mother, matrix of all phenomena,
manifests as your six-wheeled chariot:
this subtle body, composed of radiance,
that contains six ascending levels of consciousness.

The primordial currents of bright energy
    in this precious human body
are reins fastened to the root awareness.
The charioteer is the awakened, skillful practitioner
    who guides this luminous vehicle
from one dimension of reality to the next,
assisted by the five senses in transcendental form
    as Warrior Goddesses of wisdom.
The matched pair of powerful horses,
union of masculine and feminine energy,
gallop and prance with ecstasy
    in the timeless light of ultimacy.
Yet these magnificent steeds can barely move
    when the chariot is thrown out of harmony.

Pilgrimage to external shrines is fruitless effort,
merely traveling divergent roads.
One should not be anxious to wander about.
O longing mind, awaken at the confluence
    of three holy rivers.
Swim joyfully here in pristine waters of clarity
    at the source of the subtle body.

When the five elements that compose my intricate form
    separate and return to their original state,
this poet will exist solely as Mother.

Invoke immediately the revelatory
Kali, Kali, Kali
with the full force of your capacity!
O foolish mind, time is running away.

O meditator, become the Goddess

O compassionate Tara,
your radiant presence is my essence.
O Mother Kundalini,
coiled potency arising gradually
    as consciousness within all beings,
you abide in the primal root of awareness,
four petals at the base of the spine,
and within the thousand-petal lotus
    that blossoms at the crown.

The inward river Ganga flows through
    right-hand regions as molten sun,
inward river Jumna through
    left-hand regions as liquid moon.
The central stream of your energy, O Kundalini,
is luminous clarity, the inward river Saraswati,
union of Mother Reality and Father Reality.

Assuming form as the serpent of self-luminosity
    at rest in red coils about Lord Shiva,
who is the clear light of contemplation,
you awaken and manifest, O Mother,
on the petals of six ascending lotus centers
    as the fifty letters of the sacred alphabet.
Your dynamic power alone plays through solar plexus,
focus of strength and will.
Seed sounds of your feminine mystery
    balance on twelve petals of the lotus heart.
Your potent vowels cluster
    on the sixteen-petal lotus at the throat.
Syllables containing your revolutionary wisdom
    emanate from the two-petal lotus
between the eyebrows.

My beloved mentor once whispered in my ear
    these instructions for meditation:
"Visualize your own body
    as sparkling Goddess energy.
Within six spirals of consciousness,
the universal form of humanity,
dwells every being from the heavenly hierarchy
    embodying feminine or masculine energy,
each riding an animal that manifests power or beauty:
elephant, bull, ram, lion, peacock, swan, deer.
When breath catches in delight
    and enters momentary suspension,
these subtle structures flash before the inner eye
    and sweet humming music is heard:
first the bass note of a black bee
    intoxicated by golden pollen,
then waves roaring in the conscious ocean.

"Ascend swiftly in awareness through six levels,
symbolized by dense earth, flowing water,
dancing fire, invisible wind, open space,
and all-embracing mind,
each one entered with a key of sacred sound.

"Emerging into her thousand-petal reality,
O meditator, become the Goddess consciously.
She is your essence, you her expression.
Now cast your burning glance of compassion
    upon all beings in creation.
You are the primal sound
    that pervades all phenomena,
you the pearl of clear light beyond all worlds.
You bear a snow-white skull cup like the half-moon,
brimming with the nectar of timeless bliss.
You flash the curving sword of nondual wisdom.
No boundary can now remain."

There is only consciousness.
Who can create division?
Methods of prayer and meditation are numerous,
but there need be no concern over this.
All sacred ways are simply
        the free play of Goddess Kali
through diverse modes of longing.
The soul who awakens as her reality
        never falls asleep again
into waking dreams of conflict and separation.
The awakened soul disappears into its source.
Can one return into the realm of egocentric desire,
captivated by pleasure or bounded by fear,
after plunging into boundless space?

O Goddess, now open the brilliant lotus
        behind the human brow
and remove every sorrow from your lovers.
Please unite your ascending creative energy
        with your eternal clear light
that shines from the thousand-petal lotus of reality,
source of the six-lotus human body.
Light and light alone abides here
        as *Kali, Kali, Kali.*

Any person of mystic inclination
        who hears this poet's awakened cry
will swim in the limitless sea of ecstasy,
ocean of illumination
        that receives all conscious streams.

This is no ordinary wine I am drinking

This is no ordinary wine I am drinking.
I imbibe only the nectar of timeless awareness
    and lose myself while chanting:
"Victory to Kali! *Jai Ma Kali!*
Victory over the illusion of negativity!"

The divinely inebriating Goddess energy
    now permeates this poet so completely
that common drunkards, soaked in wine,
embrace me as their intimate companion.
To ingest substances that stimulate
    mundane body and mundane mind
does not make one a worshiper of Kali the Sublime.
Who can comprehend the secret
    behind the ancient ceremony
that transmutes wine into the Great Cause?
Only her lovers genuinely mad with longing
    can really know and really be.

The wine of love is distilled most carefully
    from the constant repetition *Kali, Kali, Kali,*
breath infused with Mother energy.
The sweet nectar is then steeped over
    the modulated fire of passion and desire
by the Goddess who brews this drink of nonduality
    that has transformed me so entirely.
While repeating *Om Kali, Om Kali,*
drink deep, O mind, drink deep!

This inconceivably drunken poet sings:
"If you imbibe ambrosia
    streaming from the highest lotus center,
you will attain righteousness, abundance,
delight, and illumination,
the indivisible wholeness, Mother Wisdom."

Who cares for traveling?

Who cares for traveling
　　to every sacred planetary place?
I simply long to breathe with each breath,
as though it were my last,
　　Ma Kali, Ma Kali, Ma Kali.

Does the person imbued with Goddess reality,
who breathes her name of power constantly,
feel any need for elaborate forms
　　of prayer, worship, meditation?
Even if the very principle of contemplation
　　went searching for this elusive child of Mother,
no trace would ever be found.

The indrawn mind of such a lover
　　becomes allergic to religious formality:
animal sacrifice, self-conscious charity,
plucking flowers, decorating images,
telling beads, repeating formulas.
Free from static meditation,
this poet's only sacrifice and offering
　　is to give away all sense of separate being
at the radiant feet of the universal Mother.

Who can imagine the transforming power
　　of her glorious name?
Even Shiva, bright essence of divinity,
chants *Kali, Kali, Kali*
　　with the full force of his intensity,
enabling him to drink the negativity
　　arising from countless egocentric beings,
the saving act that turns his throat
　　dark Kali-blue.

Can anyone tell me why tears stream from these eyes?

Can anyone tell me why tears stream from these eyes
    whenever I sing Ma Kali's name?
O mind, you are the vast reservoir of experience
    and the instrument of her wisdom.
Please penetrate the cause of this phenomenon
    and bring me understanding.

The mundane body is like damp wood, O friend,
soaked by the rain of worldliness.
The roaring fire *Kali, Kali, Kali,*
spreading from tongue to limbs to other organs,
drives forth this moisture as a flood of tears.

When you concentrate profoundly,
opening your inward eye in meditative gaze,
envision the holy river that is the universe
    streaming through Shiva's matted locks
and perceive the Goddess as a bright black flame,
dancing freely on his snow-white form.

The whirling spirals of consciousness,
at the base of the spine and between the eyebrows,
unite three rivers of Goddess energy:
Ganga, Jumna, and Saraswati.
With inconceivable intensity,
Mother Kundalini flows through this landscape,
the magnificent human body.

Her aspiring poet pleads:
"O pure mind, O cherished friend,
please bring me to your secluded hermitage
    overlooking the confluence
where triple nerve channels meet and merge,
close to Mother's thousand-petal lotus sea."

Who is this Supreme Lady, victorious in battle?

The face of the Goddess is an immaculate moon.
She is always transported by bliss,
inebriated by the nectar of her own mystery.
Even the force of eros trembles when it glimpses
    her enthralling form.
Lord Shiva, sovereign of wisdom,
who is one with Absolute Reality,
expires in ecstasy at her feet of beauty.
Who is this Supreme Lady, victorious in battle,
her living light streaming throughout the cosmos?
Smiling delicately as the crescent moon,
she causes every being
    to taste its own innate delight,
nondual awareness.

O meditator, hold this astonishing feminine presence
    at the center of consciousness.
Her three eyes
    are the moon of tenderness, the sun of power,
and the cosmic wisdom fire that dissolves the universe.
Her gaze creates a lover's intimacy.
This Warrior Woman, fountain of blessing,
whose daughter is she?
What motive draws her into this battlefield,
this vast display of universal suffering?

Demons of ego are arrayed against her,
faces distorted by rage,
fingernails like winnowing hooks,
teeth resembling bloodstained roots,
hair dusty with the madness of arrogance,
limbs grimy with cruel negation.

This trembling poet weeps:
"Deliver, O Kali, from egocentric obsession
    this child who repeats *Ma, Ma, Ma,*
dreading the forces of delusion that threaten
    your precious spiritual children.
O Warrior Goddess,
if you do not transform this negative energy
    with your sword of mercy
and the alchemy of your terrible beauty,
who will be left to call you Mother?"

Please cherish no hope for this poet

The awesome name Ma Kali
    steals away mundane power and prosperity
from the lives of her ecstatic lovers,
leaving only tattered wearing cloth,
and eventually not even that.
As concentrated flame
    purifies gold from dross,
so the fire of your name, O Wisdom Mother,
dissolves worldly magnificence,
leaving just the simplicity of existence,
the essence of awareness.

Frightened by the dangers of earthly life,
your children utter *Kali, Kali, Kali,*
and you respond instantly,
revealing your powerful presence in their hearts.
This presence gradually becomes all-consuming.

O Goddess, how can your children
    sustain a life of mere convention,
whether at home or in a monastery,
when Divine Mother and Divine Father
    wander through the landscape of open space,
banyan trees for shelter, cremation grounds for sanctuary,
their naked radiance concealed entirely
    beneath ashes of total renunciation?
Ma! Ma! Ma!
Give us a taste for nonduality only!

Kali encircles, enthralls,
and consumes the singer of this song,
who cries at last:
"It is impossible now to find me.

O sisters and brothers, friends of truth,
please cherish no hope for this poet,
who is lost completely
    to the world of individuality."

Radiant Uma is no ordinary girl

Radiant Uma is no ordinary girl.
O King Himalaya, she is not just your daughter
    as sacred myth describes her.
This poet sings only what is ultimately true.

How can I dare to express the exaltedness of Uma
    revealed in transcendental vision?
I am suddenly in ecstasy.
The powerful trinity of Divine Beings,
each with four faces symbolic of totality,
carry her delicate form
    upon their heads most humbly
while Uma, who is supreme,
smiles as she discourses on inexpressible mystery.

With vivid intensity my dream still shines.
Divine Perfection as the beautiful dark Vishnu,
riding the great golden warrior bird Garuda,
comes to request her blessing,
his palms together in prayerful adoration.

This inebriated poet laughs and exclaims:
"O mystic Mountain,
gaze once more at your amazing daughter!
She is the eternal dawning of nondual wisdom.
Sages rarely glimpse her formless form
    in their most profound meditation.
Even Shiva cannot comprehend her
    from his state of total absorption."

My darling, my beloved one, you have come!

"O queen, rise up from your earthly throne.
Word spreads like fire through the kingdom
    that your daughter Uma,
emanation of Divine Reality,
is now approaching the capital city."

"O loyal handmaiden,
what bliss you have ignited in my inward being!
In exchange for these tidings
    I would offer my very soul.
Choose any of the royal treasures,
or accept instead my heart of love,
for only the most precious jewel
    can repay my spiritual debt to you."

Overwhelmed with rapture,
queen mother races to meet her daughter,
who is Mother of the Universe.
The queen's formal tresses tumble
    from the crown of her head
as she forgets the entire conventional realm.
Lost in sweet madness, drenched in tears,
barefoot sovereign asks every humble person
    along the central thoroughfare
how close her Golden One has come
    to the gates of relative existence.
As earthly queen moves among her swirling populace,
the royal chariot of Mother Reality
    arrives spontaneously.
The enlightened face of Uma,
beheld suddenly by awestruck humanity,
is the full moon of nonduality.

The queen can only cry in ecstasy:
"My darling, my beloved one, you have come!

Most precious Uma, my life and joy!
Have you forgotten this mortal being
    who gave you physical incarnation?"

The Goddess in human form responds gently:
"Dearest mother, what are you saying?
How can I forget you?"
Uma alights and makes obeisance,
touching her mother's dusty feet
    in purity of heart,
consoling the tearful queen
    with unimaginable tenderness.

This poet and servant of Mother
    is awed, humbled, and can barely form words:
"Who? Who? Who?
Who in this world has ever witnessed
    such profound auspiciousness,
such intimacy with Divine Reality?"

Speak wisdom to us, sweet Uma

"O queen among women,
the unique day of radiance has dawned.
Your daughter Uma, Divine Mother incarnate,
is arriving for her yearly visit.
Abandon every duty and welcome her home.
Come forth from the world of convention
    and gaze upon her transcendent face,
the perpetual full moon of wisdom,
the brilliance of open space.
The suffering of illusory separation
    will gradually dissolve,
as the moonlight of her smile
    floods the human dimension."

Hearing this intense call,
queen mother runs from her palace in ecstasy,
cloth unraveling, tears flying,
long hair streaming free.
Her entire being permeated by holy affection,
turning her back on finite king and kingdom,
she plunges into Uma's infinite embrace,
weeping with a selfless joy
    the egocentric world has never known.

Human mother sits beside Divine Daughter,
gazing into her luminous eyes
    and kissing her sacred lips
that attract those who long for pure being
    like bees drawn to a crimson blossom.

Breathlessly, limited queen
    addresses limitless Sovereign:
"Most precious Uma, crest-jewel among women,
though wealthy King Himalaya is your father,
your husband, Shiva, is a wandering ascetic.

173

How could I have married my beautiful royal daughter
    to one clothed only in ashes and sky?"

Uma's childhood playmates,
now mature women,
intimate with her, laughing with rapture,
kiss her healing hands and inquire:
"Did you remember us during your wandering?
Speak wisdom to us, sweet Uma.
The light of our hearts is obscured
    by the gloom of habit and convention."

This divinely drunken poet
    now brims with laughter,
swims in the ocean of bliss,
and sings through tears:
"When Goddess manifests through human form,
awareness overflows with pure delight.
No longer recognizing day or night,
the soul disappears into her reality.
Even ecstasy is forgotten completely."

Blessed baby Uma is weeping constantly

"O noble King Himalaya,
this human mother cannot console the Divine Mother
    miraculously manifest as our child.
Blessed baby Uma is weeping constantly
    with spiritual longing.
She takes no delight in relative existence,
refusing to accept her mother's breast.
She will not even touch butter or cream.

"Uma remains awake throughout the night,
and when the moon rises, she gazes intensely.
Sometimes she pleads: *Catch it for me!*
Her delicate eyes are swollen with crying,
her radiant face is pale.
How can a mother's heart bear this sight?
Desperately, she repeats: *Ma, Ma, Ma.*
Grasping my fingers in her tiny hand,
she cries: *Come with me now! Please come!*
I have no idea where she wants to go.
When I try to explain to her
    that moon and earth can never meet,
she discards her clothing and pushes me away."

Now the King of Mystic Mountains
    receives shining Uma in his arms
and holds the Golden One with awe and tenderness.
Inspired by the bliss of her holy touch,
he offers a small mirror
    and speaks in gentle tones:
"Enjoy this moon on earth, my sweetest child."
Uma enters ecstasy at the sight of her own face,
more brilliant than a sky full of moons.

Before tear-filled eyes of mother and father,
this full incarnation of Goddess energy,
released from excruciating longing
     by the vision of her own reality,
falls deep into the sleep of meditation.
With indescribable love, human mother
     bears luminous form of Divine Mother
to her small chamber.

This poet is touched to the core:
"How infinitely blessed are those parents
     to whom the Mother of the Universe is born!"

How sweetly baby Uma repeats Ma, Ma, Ma

May we stroll to the banks
    of the majestic river of mystic union,
and with its sacred water offer worship
    to the Goddess of Wisdom in human form.

Listen, queen mother, to this rare music,
your Divine Daughter cooing joyfully,
her golden face suffused
    with a smile of holy ecstasy.
Her tones are more melodious than birdsong,
the blessing of her presence more refreshing
    than the cool breeze from Mother Ganga.
How sweetly baby Uma repeats *Ma, Ma, Ma,*
invoking her own infinity.
The dazzling peacock pales beside her radiance.
Full moon appears dim and lily dull
    in the light of her resplendent reality.

The words of my song stand utterly destitute
    before her divine beauty.
This impoverished poet of Mother can only cry:
"O Goddess, who incarnates gracefully
    as Uma the Beloved,
you are known to be intensely merciful
    to poor ones who love only you.
Please save me from the implacable ocean
    of impermanence and suffering.
Save me, Ma! Lift me up!
A single glance from your tender human eyes
    can enlighten all living beings!"

Please meditate on Goddess Kali's beauty ceaselessly

The Supreme Lady stands magnificently
    on the breast of transcendent Reality,
who is her mystic consort, supine, dead to relativity.
Bloodstreams of countless beings adorn her black form
    as streaks of lightning pervade a dark thundercloud.
How utterly inconceivable is she!
The very touch of her dancing feet
    has plunged Shiva, the Cosmic Dancer,
into bright, still, formless ecstasy.

She is the free play of love,
unveiling universal manifestation.
Shiva is her own hiddenness,
her secret nature as absolutely unmanifest.
Her two eyes stream with power and compassion,
rising sun and full moon that float in one black sky.
Her brow bears a third eye of wisdom
    like the crescent moon,
perceiving past and future
    as timeless transparency.
Her form arises spontaneously,
a single moon more vast than the cosmic sea.
Her feet are mountains of ordinary moons.
Rich fragrance streams
    from her beautiful darkness.
She moves with the elephant's earth-shaking grace.

This ecstatic lover, whom some have called
    the mad poet of the Mother,
now cries out to all humanity:
"O lovers of truth! Sisters and brothers!
Please meditate on Goddess Kali's beauty ceaselessly
    by night and day,
singing *Kali, Kali, Kali.*"

My precious human birth has been wasted utterly

Who is this transcendent woman
    striding across the heart of Absolute Reality?
Her sublime form, darker than the darkest thunderhead,
streams with all blood ever shed.
Fingernails and toenails are crescent moons
    floating in the midnight sky.
Skin delicate as a dark blue lotus,
drops of perspiration adorn her body,
pearls rolling across a sapphire mirror.

Her beauty is enthralling, annihilating.
Tangled strands of her hair flow wildly
    like the blackness of the breaking storm,
dispelling with their dark luminosity
    all despair and negativity.
Her thundering steps overwhelm
    cosmic serpent and cosmic tortoise
at the foundation of the universe,
and even they are plunged into timeless trance.

Why is this careless poet lover
    still distracted from her grandeur
by the petty diversion of egocentric pleasure,
failing to remember the Goddess ceaselessly?
Her hopeless bard laments:
"Such is the strange destiny
    of one who sings Mother's songs
yet fails to realize her profoundly.
My precious human birth
    has been wasted utterly."

179

Abandon whatever limits you cling to

Kali is naked reality.
She is the feminine principle, unifying wisdom.
This simpleminded lover of truth
    calls her *my Mother, my Mother,*
because she is the inexhaustible affection
    who never neglects her children,
no matter how heedless or rebellious they may be.

Wisdom Mother cares for this child
    more tenderly than human mother,
yet her creative and destructive actions
    are startling, wild, unpredictable
as those of a mad person.
She is surrounded by swirling energy,
manifest in various feminine forms
    as human beings and etheric beings:
powerful women warriors, peaceful contemplatives,
terrifying protectresses surrounded by flames.
Godhead in its three aspects,
Creator, Sustainer, and Revealer,
stands humbly before my Mother.
She is supreme.

This poet urges every human heart:
"If you wish to be liberated from oppression,
abandon whatever limits you cling to
    and meditate on the limitless one
who wears limitation as a garland of heads
    severed by her sword of nondual wisdom."

Give up your hopeless dispute with Kali

I am entirely lost in awe!
Who is the inexhaustible fountain of being
    that enchants every mind?
Who is the origin of this boundless ecstasy
    that enraptures every heart?
She is Kali! She is Kali!
Her constant stream of lightning flashes
    are facets of a single spinning diamond.
Inexorably the Supreme Lady
    attracts awareness to its timeless core,
dissolving the demons of negativity,
withdrawing the illusion of separation and division.

The dark blue lotus blossom
    is nothing before her beauty.
The crest jewel of nondual wisdom
    shines on her forehead like the full moon.
She stands poised on the breast of Transcendence,
needing no male companion to protect her
    in the battlefield of universal suffering.
Sacred streaks of white sandal paste
    scintillate upon her noble black brow.
Sparkling gemstones swing from her nose ring
    as she dances, whirling and smiling.

I am overwhelmed!
She is beautiful! So beautiful!
Her gaze is a bubbling spring of ambrosia
    that brings instantaneous delight.
Behold her and beware, O King of Demons,
principle of egocentricity and bitter negation!

Surrounded by dynamic maidens
    who bear her wisdom weapons,

she laughs aloud, regarding relative existence
    as one vast cremation ground.
Her long hair swirls
    like a giant tree in a midnight gale.
The sublime Warrior Woman crushes demonic forces
    and grants her own great bliss
to those who join her selflessly
    in ecstatic warfare against negativity.

This poet empowered by the Goddess
    boldly addresses the Demon King
who hides deep within the human mind:
"O Monarch of Misery,
give up your hopeless dispute with Kali.
I am no longer under the illusion of your rule,
knowing her alone to be my essence.
You will never taste victory.
Submit your entire being to her tender mercy,
simply by uttering *Kali, Kali, Kali.*"

None will survive the fury of her illumination

I am overcome with sacred terror!
Before me stands the supreme warrior!
The cosmos quakes beneath her stamping feet
     as she directly confronts the forces of negation.
Chariots and drivers, horses and horsemen,
arrows and archers she devours whole.
Divine body blacker than the King of Death,
timelessness shines from her forehead.
Her flying hair veils the sun.
Moon falls to earth in swoon.
Elephants of war stampede and are lost in her
     as moths consumed by flame.

The incomparable light of Kali's beauty
     pervades the universe
as she swallows into her dazzling darkness
     the ferocious army of demonic passions.
Her boon companion, warrior maiden Bhairavi,
strikes her powerful cheeks like drums.
Her intimate helper, wisdom maiden Yogini,
claps her hands in rhythmic ecstasy
     to Kali's high-pitched cry of victory.
My mind is transformed by the strange sweetness
     of these thrilling sounds.

Beside Ma Kali stands a peaceful maiden
     who bears her chalice of timeless awareness.
The Black Queen now dances gracefully,
her smile more brilliant than the full moon.
She has destroyed the narrow hopes
     of every limited self in creation
by consuming objective and subjective worlds
     in ecstatic conflagration.

All beings must now renounce
    conventional projects and projection.
None will survive the fury of her illumination.

This poet sings the truth
    that is most revolutionary:
"By uttering *Ma Kali, Ma Kali,*
the soul completes its pilgrimage instantly,
forever one with Mother Reality."

Stop! Stop! Cease and be still!

Complexion more radiant than the royal-blue lotus,
her long black hair flows perfectly free.
Who is she? Who is she?
Body not protected by armor or garments,
she stands in the chaos of conflict fearlessly.
She is primordial beauty.
The loveliness of her breasts
    consumes every limited gaze
in the fire of naked luminosity.

This supreme lady, Mother Reality,
moves with dramatic stride and brilliant smile.
Like devastating thunder
    at the dissolution of the universe,
her cry of truth sounds forth:
Stop! Stop! Cease and be still!

Her vibrant presence enchants
    the heart and mind of every being,
yet she remains sublimely terrifying,
as though sister to Death,
transforming into profound humility
    the pride of those who oppose her foolishly.
Her enthusiasm for battle remains fresh,
like a warrior who has just completed training.
Her skill in combat unique and invincible,
Goddess Kali advances directly
    to the stronghold of the enemy
and stares down Death
    with her steady gaze of victory.

This poet trembles, barely able to sing:
"The realm of relative existence
    is engaged in ceaseless war.

Death is attacking with superior forces.
I cannot resist its overwhelming illusion.
My Warrior Mother alone can save me."

Conquer Death with the drumbeat Ma! Ma! Ma!

Who is this unique warrior woman?
Her terrifying war cry
    pervades the universal battleground.
Who is this incomparable feminine principle?
Contemplating her limitless nature,
the passion to possess and be gratified dissolves.
Who is this elusive wisdom woman?
Her smooth and fragrant body of intense awareness
    is like the petal of a dark blue lotus.

A single eye of knowledge
    shines from her noble forehead
like a moon so full its light engulfs the sun.
This mysterious Goddess, eternally sixteen,
is naked brilliance, transparent insight.
Cascades of black hair stream down her back
    to touch her dancing feet.
Perfect in the art of wisdom warfare,
she is the treasury of every excellence,
the reservoir of all that is good.

Her poet sings with unshakable assurance:
"Anyone who lives consciously in the presence
    of this resplendent savioress
can conquer Death with the drumbeat
    Ma! Ma! Ma!"

She is the infinite dream power of reality

Who is this mystic woman of sheer loveliness?
The harmony of her noble features
    is illumined by the mysterious glow
of the dark moon on her forehead.
Vigorously she strides
    through the battleground of relativity,
tresses of power flowing wildly,
body black as the blackest new-moon night.

Totally alive
    with the youth of timelessness,
no garment can cover or even touch her.
With two left hands she bears
    the sword of nondual wisdom
and the severed head of mundane convention.
With two right hands she demonstrates
    motherly protection and boundless generosity.
I am transported in ecstasy! I am absorbed utterly!
Unimaginable and inconceivable is her beauty!
Do you dare to gaze upon her,   .
O self-serving mind and senses?
She manifests as eternal Goddess,
etheric beings, and as earthly women.

Lord Shiva, sublime knower of reality,
fearless one on whom seekers of transcendent truth rely,
casts away his divine form at her feet of bliss.
With her indescribable love she has now destroyed
    the very Destroyer of Death.

After stealing away with the hearts of her lovers,
she disappears into a storm of transformation,
reappearing again as Cosmic Dreamer,
her enlightened laughter so intense
    it awakens sacred terror.

Racing across the green and blue planet,
she leaps into the blackness between stars,
devouring every participant
     in the war of illusory opposition:
soldiers, chariots, horses, weapons.

This awestruck poet reminds humanity:
"You know almost nothing
     concerning Mother's grandeur.
She is the infinite dream power of reality.
She is the dynamic play of pure consciousness.
The one who sports as divine love incarnate,
Krishna of the tender human heart,
is the very one who rages blissfully as Kali,
consuming names and forms entirely.
Both embody nondual wisdom.
Meditate on his flute and her sword as one!"

She is truth! She is awareness!

From deep within Shiva's secret kingdom,
knowledge of reality,
there radiates the timeless light
    of his magnificent consort Kali.
She is the royal-blue lotus that floats
    on the lake of his transcendent body.
Soles of her feet red rising suns,
toenails luminous new moons,
she stands clear and naked.
She is truth! She is awareness!

Her thighs are luxuriant
    as dark green plantain trees,
her navel deep as a reservoir.
Severed limbs of demonic passions
    and silver bells of divine remembrance
grace her shining waistband.
Her high breasts brim with the nectar
    of wisdom and compassion,
enhancing the startling beauty of her form.
Heavenly and earthly beings alike
    drink this nectar in sheer delight.
She is the very sustenance of existence.

Her mysterious function is fourfold.
One left hand holds
    the demonic head of hatred by its hair.
The other wields her merciful sword of liberation.
One right hand radiates the energy of protection.
The other grants gifts of motherly generosity.
Those who oppose her with various modes of negativity
    she subjects to abject terror.
Yet her blissful ferocity
    appears to authentic lovers as safety.
From her they taste the sweet honey of rapture.

Her countenance is overwhelming to gaze upon.
Long crimson tongue flowing from her mouth,
sparkling with the light of every sacred shrine,
she laughs with amazing intensity
    and disarming intimacy.
Goddess eyes of power and mercy
    are sun and moon in one black sky.
Third eye of wisdom is the cosmic fire
    at the end of history.
Forehead bears crescent moon
    and vermilion dot of consecration.
Earrings assume the form of dead infants,
emblem of uncompromising renunciation.
Abundant black hair that tumbles to her feet
    is her power of transformation.
Her smile is the prolonged lightning flash
    of full illumination.

Ecstatic sages circle around her sweetness
    as inebriated bees about an open lotus.
Skin fresh and dark as newly forming storm clouds,
she is the essence of beauty, earthly and heavenly.
She is royal wealth for lovers of reality.
She alone holds the key to her inconceivable treasury,
the direct experience of nonduality.
For Shiva,
she remains pure mystery.

Kali! Kali! Kali!
You destroy death's illusion!
You vanquish bodily torment,
anguish of heart, spiritual confusion!
You and you alone, O Mother,
grant freedom and illumination
    to this astonished poet lover

during waking, dream, and dreamlessness,
revealing your true nature as indivisible
    awareness and bliss.

This is the only longing of my soul

The bright black lady of supreme beauty
    strides across the immaculate breast
of the Absolute Reality that annuls negativity.
Her feet of purity are midnight sky.
Her toenails shine delicately
    with cool rays of moonlight.
Her tumultuous wisdom laughter
    dispels pervasive delusion.
Her sweet wisdom speech rains nectar
    throughout the cosmos.

Awakened souls rush toward her fragrant lips,
brilliant bees drawn by the mystic lotus.
She is the flowering of timeless awareness.
Ever young, naked, precise, alert,
thrilling and compelling to behold,
she wields her flashing diamond sword of truth
    with consummate warrior's skill.
Volleys of arrows from her bow of insight
    pierce the very heart of selfish clinging.

The poet and lover who sings this song
    cries out spontaneously:
"My eyes overflow with tears of ecstasy
    as I meditate upon the Black Goddess.
May the mind remain consecrated forever
    to her lotus feet of beautiful darkness.
This is the only longing of my soul."

Do I dare disclose her secret?

O misguided mind, are you mad?
Can you worship the Mother of the Universe
    by sitting in a dark room,
legs crossed, eyes closed, breath in suspension?
She is the play of boundless affection.
No one can realize her embracing reality
    who is not consumed by the fire of love.

Listen, O mind, to authentic instruction.
First transmute every limited, grasping love
    by evoking her luminous power
in the subtle nerve channels of this precious body.
What splendid joy to discover that she alone
    abides in the central chamber of your house,
waking at midnight and sleeping after dawn,
she who cannot be comprehended
    by any system of philosophy,
who is beyond cosmic science,
who transcends even secret teaching.

Supreme principle of pure love,
free from limits of subject or object,
she resides in the royal palace of the subtle body,
dancing wildly, then gently,
every mood absorbed in timeless bliss.
She is the sole practitioner of mystic union
    whose very being is the ecstasy of unity.
She alone is the one who meditates through aspirants
    who belong to every spiritual way.
Whenever profound love matures within a human heart,
she draws it consciously into her heart.
The invisible pole always
    attracts the shining needle of the compass.

This poet who remains focused only on Mother
    sings breathlessly:
"Do I dare disclose her secret?
She has become my very body!
Even this is only a hint, O mind.
There is nothing apart from her reality."

I am gone, gone, forever gone

This foolish poet who sings
    to the Mother of the Universe
has finally comprehended
    the secret of spiritual practice.
Recognize your very existence,
no matter how you live,
as her changeless diamond nature.

This supremely radical teaching
    is revealed from the ground of being,
Lord Shiva, primordial and pristine,
by the perpetual lightning flash,
Goddess Reality.
Lovers who travel her way beyond meditation
    receive all-embracing Mother Wisdom,
empowering the mind to discard completely
    every egocentric attraction or repulsion
by focusing awareness solely
    on its own innate purity,
its natural self-luminosity.

Treasure with constant care,
in the thousand-petal lotus at the crown,
the mystic sound of liberation,
Mother Kali's potent name.
Breathe with every breath
    the sound of transformation,
Om Kali Ma.

This poet, no longer lost and wandering,
now sings with adamantine conviction:
"I know without doubt
    my culminating journey has begun.

Kali, Kali, Kali
    is my sole provision.
I am gone, gone, forever gone."

Awake, arise, and never rest

O drowsy mind,
awaken to your intrinsic clarity.
Sing lucid songs of victory to Goddess Kali.
O habitually wandering mind,
do not slide into sleep imperceptibly
	or you will forget the innate treasure,
your own radiant diamond nature.

If you become comfortable
	upon the bed of forgetfulness
in the nine-door chamber of the human body,
the clever thieves of egocentric craving
	will break in easily
and steal your precious spiritual energy.

Through the power of my Mother,
this poet of awakening sings with vigor:
"Awake, arise, and never rest
	until the day of illumination dawns
for every conscious being in the universe."

The play of my soul is over

O blissful Mother,
the play of my soul is over.
My strange dream of action and passion
    is now complete.
Ma! Ma! Ma!
I took this incarnation
    to experience your universal drama,
yet like a small child,
I only played with dust.

O Daughter of the Sacred Mountain,
fountain of self-luminosity,
at this pregnant moment
    you have brought death near me.
My childhood passed in playfulness,
my later years were games of limited love,
and now age has slowed my steps
    till I no longer dance with delusion.

This poet supplicates ceaselessly:
"Holy Mother! Holy Mother!
Grant me pure love for you only!
Merge me irretrievably
    into your beautiful black mystery."

May I now become dust beneath my Holy Mother's feet!

Goddess Kali,
you must listen to my story!
Although awakened souls experience you
    as tender compassion,
I encounter you only as impersonal power
    who grants vast wealth to some,
placing them on chariots of triumph
    attended by elephants of worldly splendor,
while for others you ordain a life of common labor,
without even greens or salt for their rice.
Only a few inhabit the jewel palace
    of ultimate realization.
To dwell in your transparent oneness
    has been my fruitless longing!

Are victorious saints alone important, Mother,
and this poor one who loves you nothing?
Some persons you clothe
    with fine woolen shawls,
and they enjoy the sweetened yogurt of devotion.
Others you allow to live on grain
    that has not been husked with care
and is mixed with the sand of rebellion.
Some persons are borne high
    on the shoulders of those who bear burdens.
I am one of your bent-over laborers!

Ma! Ma! Ma!
I carelessly neglected to reap the rich harvest
    of your unimaginable blessing.
This poet has sowed songs in vain.
I can only weep:
"By failing to remember the Goddess
    with every breath and every intention,

I have lived miserably.
May I now become dust
    beneath my Holy Mother's feet!"

Contemporary Visions of the Goddess

SOME REFLECTIONS ON RAMPRASAD

BY SHUMA CHAKRAVARTY

*L*ike most poets and visionaries, Ramprasad's life is jeweled with myths and metaphors. Amidst a wealth of paradoxes, one must ponder which aspects can be selected to form a plausible biographical sketch.

Ramprasad Sen was born in 1723 in Bengal, in the village of Halishawhar (also called Kumarhati). His father's name was Ramram Sen, and his mother was called Siddheswari Devi. Ramprasad had several siblings. He was married at the age of twenty-two to a maiden called Sarvani. She was a devoted wife, and they became the parents of several children.

Ramprasad's father was an Ayurvedic doctor and had hoped that his son would follow his profession. But Ramprasad was an otherworldly mystic and poet. From a very young age, he was an impassioned lover of God as Divine Mother. His parents tried, without success, to interest him in practical subjects and skills. He was given a good education and encouraged to express his talents. He learned Persian and Hindi with ease. Thus, he could have earned a living as a translator in the courts of Muslim leaders of India in the mid-eighteenth century. Instead, he used his linguistic gifts to deepen his knowledge and love of mystical literature.

When Ramprasad was still a boy, he was initiated into religious practices by his family's mentor/guru. After the sudden demise of that teacher, a famous tantric sage called Agambagish came to the village of Kumarhati and was impressed by Ramprasad's spiritual depth. Agambagish spent a few days instructing Ramprasad about the nuances of the tantric path. This path is the complete union of human and Divine, experienced directly in the subtle body. Ramprasad's parents were pleased by their son's complete absorption in spiritual ideals and his indifference to worldly issues. They found consolation in believing that God would somehow provide for their small, poor family, since Ramprasad did not seem to be a likely candidate for the role of breadwinner. However, the death of his father placed the responsibility of providing for the family squarely on the shoulders of Ramprasad. He left his village and became a clerk in Calcutta in the household of Durgacharan Mitra. His monthly salary was Rs. 30 (or $1). Ramprasad was both delighted and relieved to have found employment. His gratitude and joy took the form of poems in praise of Goddess Kali, Mother of the Universe. His fellow employees were aghast to see Ramprasad using his account book for the composition of these hymns. Their complaints eventually led to Ramprasad being summoned by their employer. Ramprasad went to see his boss, Durgacharan, ledger in hand. When Durgacharan Mitra read the inspired songs composed by Ramprasad, he was moved by his clerk's piety and impressed by his literary genius. He granted Ramprasad leave to return to his native village and promised the poet that he would be paid his salary every month in order to continue writing.

On different occasions, both a Hindu king, Raja Krishnachandra, and a Muslim prince, Sirajuddullah, were inspired by Ramprasad's songs and wanted him to be a court musician. Ramprasad declined both offers. But Raja Krishnachandra gave Ramprasad a hundred acres of land, and the poet, in return, dedicated his book *Vidyasundar* (Beautiful Knowledge) to this Hindu ruler. As a courtesy to Sirajuddullah, Ramprasad is believed to have visited him once in Murshidabad, in response to the Muslim prince's fervent request. Evidently, Ramprasad's mystical attainments were also recognized by Sufis. At the end of Raja Krishnachandra's life, it was Ramprasad who helped him make his transition peacefully by singing Kali songs at his deathbed.

One of the many revelatory events associated with Ramprasad's life is an encounter with Divine Mother while he was repairing a fence. At first, his daughter was assisting him; then the child went away. However, a radiant girl came, helped him complete the task, and then vanished. Only later, he realized that he had enjoyed a waking vision of Goddess Kali.

Ramprasad spent his life absorbed in spiritual practices and contemplative moods. His creative gift was like a flowing fountain. Today only two hundred and fifty out of a reputed hundred thousand Ramprasad hymns to the Divine Mother survive, but they are an eloquent testimony to his mystical genius. There were, of course, later imitators of his work; one in particular was Ramprasad Chakravarty of Calcutta, who was thirty years younger than the saint. By the atmosphere of spiritual realization generated by Ramprasad's songs, the two poets can be easily distinguished. Aju Goswami, who was a neighbor and contemporary of Ramprasad Sen and a devotee of Krishna, not Kali, often tried to demean the poet by satirizing his songs.

The facts and legends that surround Ramprasad can only give us a faint outline of the life of this remarkable soul. However, what ensures his immortality in the land of his birth is the indisputable fact that his songs are still an integral part of the rich, vibrant spiritual life of Bengal. During a recent visit to Bengal, I heard Ramprasad's songs broadcast over the radio and sung on the streets and in the homes and temples of Calcutta by a cross-section of people—children, the elderly, housewives, businessmen, scholars, the illiterate, monks, householders, and the youth of all classes. Bengal is a bastion of poetry and Kali worship. Therefore, it is not surprising that the ineffable fusion of both in Ramprasad's work is a continuing source of inspiration to many lovers of truth and beauty who are devoted to God as the Great Mother—Goddess Kali.

Ramprasad's Muse

Goddess Kali, Ramprasad's muse and the central figure in his life, can be frightening at first glance. She is depicted in sacred iconography as black or blue-black, naked, with long, disheveled hair, carrying a sword in one hand and a severed head in another. Her waist is encircled by a band of human hands. But her two other hands carry benign signals to suffering humanity—one beckons *come unto me* and the other gestures *fear not*. She is also seen standing on the reclining body of Shiva, the transcendent, transforming aspect of Divinity, while enacting her cosmic dance.

Such a vision of Divine Reality eludes definition, and the fact that Kali is widely worshiped in India, particularly in West Bengal, may bewilder non-Hindus and some Hindus as well. Perhaps the harsh realities of famine, homelessness, disease, death, and natural disasters such as droughts, floods, earthquakes, and tidal waves have forged a deep realism about life's suffering in the inherently mystical and poetic people of Bengal. Hence, merely a serene depiction of Ultimate Reality would not be congruent with their profound experiences of life. Mother Kali is worshiped by her devotees as the Source of All, the creatrix and destroyer of limited existence as we know it. She is dark in color because God is the supreme mystery, defying all human definitions. She is represented as naked to indicate that human notions of ornament, propriety, and artifice do not apply to the Divine. Instead of ascribing the shadow side of life to Satan and only sweetness and radiance to God, Hindus see in Kali the paradox of life itself—pleasure and pain, creation and destruction, life and death. Kali is benign, beautiful, *and* terrifying, as is her creation, which Hindus call the *lila* or cosmic drama of the Great Goddess. Her sword cuts the bonds of delusion, such as lust, anger, greed, pride, and possessiveness. The severed head in one of her hands and her waistband of human hands symbolize the death of narcissism and the surrender of the fruits of our actions, sweet and bitter, to the ultimate source, who is God/Goddess.

Sri Ramakrishna (1836–1886) taught that Kali is imaged as dark because humans distance Divine Reality from their consciousness through fear and ignorance. He pointed out that the ocean also looks black or blue-black from a distance. But when we approach the ocean and scoop up a handful of water, it is experienced as clear and colorless. Similarly, when one approaches Kali very intimately, one encounters radiance, clarity, and God's unconditional love for us all.

In January 1993 it was my joy and privilege to visit the ancient Kali shrine of Kalighat in Calcutta for the dawn worship with Lex Hixon and his family. Lex and I also went to Belur Math, the monastic center of the Ramakrishna Mission, near Calcutta, on the banks of the Ganges River. We went to Kalighat and Belur Math as pilgrims, with prayerful resonance and respect for the tradition of devotion to Kali, as expressed and experienced by Ramprasad and Sri Ramakrishna. We have also participated together in the spiritual atmosphere of prayerful worship and meditation at the Vedanta Center in Cohasset, Massachusetts. This Center was founded in 1909 by Swami Paramananda, who was a disciple of Swami Vivekananda and therefore in the direct, spiritual transmission of Sri Ramakrishna. Swami Paramananda's special ideal was Mother Kali. When he passed away in 1940, he had not been able to express this ideal publicly in the context of a spiritually conservative American culture. He himself regularly sang Ramprasad's songs during his own personal devotions. How surprised and delighted he would be to see Lex Hixon's eloquent explorations of Ramprasad's songs widely read in the West. They are a truly sensitive expression of the Goddess's mysterious presence. Lex Hixon is uniquely gifted in comprehending both the literary, as well as the mystical nuances of Ramprasad's work.

While conducting the worship of Kali in Cohasset, I, too, have experienced, at times, the translucence of accord with Divinity that occurs in moments of her grace. I offer the following poem, composed on Kali Puja, November 13, 1993, in prayerful homage to Ramprasad's muse, the Mother of the Universe.

Though all else pall, pale,
and pass away,
you remain my
essential witness,
conscience, compass,
road, God, and goad.

Though today's tinsel
be tomorrow's trash,
today's ally, tomorrow's
hasty, hostile stranger,
you remain my solace
and succor, my light
and life.

Though today's drama
enchants and entraps me,
I know that
my oasis lies
only in you.

Beyond this passing
pageant of props
and power;
beyond the quicksands
of lust and greed,
the parade, charade,
passing propaganda
of vendors and panderers,
you and only you remain,
my rest and refuge,
solace and succor,
source and resource,
closest kin and
lasting friend.

210

Only you, my good and God!

You and only you
are my
vine and vindicator,
though all else
pale, pall,
and pass away.
You and only
you remain
my essential
witness,
my life, lover,
conscience, compass,
road, goad,
and God.

Author's Note:

I am indebted to Swami Bamdevananda's excellent Bengali book *Sadhak Ramprasad* (published in Calcutta by Udbodhan Press) for his valuable scholarly commentaries. This book was reprinted for the ninth time in 1986 and is still in print. It contains all Ramprasad's extant poems/songs in the original Bengali.

Editor's Note:

Shuma Chakravarty was born in Calcutta and spent her early years there. She is the assistant minister at the Vedanta Center in Cohasset, MA, and is also a Unitarian Universalist minister. She has a graduate degree in English literature from Simmons College, Boston, and two graduate degrees in theology from Boston University and Harvard. She has worked for five years as a teaching assistant to Nobel laureate Elie Wiesel. She defines herself as poet, pilgrim, and pastor, but her primary identity is that of a mystic and lover of the Divine.

DANCING WITH MOTHER KALI

BY CASSIA BERMAN

O Mother,
    who wears as a necklace
    the severed heads of the egos
    and busy minds
    of your beloved ones,
please add mine to your collection,
cut off my head with your sharp sword of mercy
so I can truly say
what needs to be said here,
so I can truly say everywhere
what needs to be said.
And where words aren't useful
may your presence shine through them anyway
so that without even needing to know what's being done
I can be secure that you use this voice of mine
to bring healing and comfort and alignment and wisdom
to each one these words reach,
wherever, whoever they are.

                                     —C.B.

I've lived with the poems in this book for more than five years, through countless revisions by the author, through changes in my own life, and through the ever-deepening and expansive process of learning who and what the Divine Mother is and who I am in relation to her. These poems cover many of the moods we human beings experience and show us how to refer everything we think and feel to the Mother to be transmuted into wisdom, truth, and reality. I've read them to groups of people and shared the excitement with which both women and men have received them. I've used them as inspiration and powerful medicine for myself. They have become part of the very fabric of my life. The goddess of these poems is infinitely powerful, beautiful, terrifying, and free, and so it is the beauty, power, and terror she awakens in me, and the call to freedom, that I write about here.

BEAUTY

> *If you wish to be liberated from oppression*
> *abandon whatever limits you cling to*
> *and meditate on the limitless one*
> *who wears limitation as a garland of heads*
> *freshly severed by her sword of nondual wisdom.*

As a child growing up Jewish in the Bronx, I learned stories from the Bible in which God spoke to people long, long ago, giving them information, guidance, and sometimes just the gift of Divine Presence. I wondered if God had stopped speaking to people at some point in time—I certainly didn't know of anyone who was having that kind of communication—but I wanted to hear that voice too, which I thought would be booming and male. When I finally heard God speak to me when I was in my late twenties, to my surprise it was in a voice that was gentle—and female! And so began my adventure with the Divine Mother, whose tradition, I learned, was still very much alive in India and can be found at the core of all of the world's cultures and spiritualities, though in our time mostly hidden by a patriarchal overlay.

Over the years, she has revealed to me with humor and grace many different aspects of herself—her beautiful faces as the goddesses of Hindu and other religions, as women of the past and present through whom she has incarnated, as a presence of light, and as a sweeter essence within me than I generally let myself feel. From each of her aspects, I've heard that gentle voice which teaches me not so much esoteric truths as very mundane lessons of being kind to myself and accepting a larger view of love and light and a more benificent universe than my perceptions would allow. Her presence, which she doesn't let me forget, has transformed my life and my being.

Even so, up until a certain point I was still a little afraid to look at her aspect called Kali—the black Hindu goddess with long red tongue who wears a garland of skulls, a waistband of human arms, and is often seen dancing on the chest of her consort Shiva, who lies beneath her feet in ecstatic surrender. And so it also came as a surprise when Mother Kali walked into my life one summer day, and I felt her as that same sweetness in my heart that I have come to associate with gentler aspects of the Divine Mother. Her entrance, I slowly realized, was but an unveiling of a power, with all her images of seeming goriness and destruction, that had always been part of my inner iconography. Opening to her touched off a series of graceful events in my life, not the least of which was meeting Lex Hixon five years ago on Kali Puja at a temple dedicated to Kali and her nineteenth-century devotees and embodiments, Ramakrishna Paramahamsa and Sri Sarada Devi. Meeting Lex there and eventually coming to assist him in a small way in his work of revealing and writing about the hidden core of feminine wisdom at the heart of sacred traditions was clearly part of Mother Kali's gift and plan for me.

POWER

> Goddess play is sheer inconceivability.
> Struggle to fathom her, O sisters and brothers,
> with every fiber of your mental energy.
> Your intelligence will be purified
>   but you will never comprehend my Mother.

Wherever one looks today, one can see the Feminine Principle striding, in all her fullness, back into all the places from which she has been exiled, demanding to be heard. Goddess worship, drawing from images of the female Deity of all times and cultures, with as many forms as we have aspects of ourselves that need celebrating, protecting, nurturing, and empowering, is in resurgence. But it is not just on an ethereal level that she is entering the world. Social and political movements which aim to restore to women a place and voice in society—from women's suffrage in the early 1900's, to the equal rights movement and its offshoots and ramifications, including the men's movement—are also evidence of the Goddess rearising. In science and medicine, advanced researchers are discovering the values of nonlinear, wholistic, intuitive modes of thinking, associated universally with the feminine principle, that take into account an indeterminacy more fitting with Eastern wisdom than with Western culture's hard-edged, rational models. Through the ecology movement, it is becoming clear to even the most insensitive that we must re-examine our relationship to Earth and nature, related to throughout the world as Mother. Movements in psychology and systems of health from the East, which picture the feminine as an energy within ourselves to be balanced, not dominated, by the masculine, are entering mainstream thought. As many proclivities as we her children have, the Mother is speaking through these varied forms—loud and clear for those who know her, secretly but relentlessly for those who do not yet—teaching us that the way we've treated our planet, ourselves, and each other is not the way a mother cares for her own.

For those who resist personification, calling this movement Mother or Goddess can be seen as a poetic device to help us make real to ourselves the essential force of life and manifestation. In Hinduism, although the Divine is one and formless, it can be symbolized as male gods representing abstract energies, who need their feminine counterparts, embodied in the goddesses, to manifest their powers. But Mother is much more than merely a female counterpart. In traditional Eastern symbolism, whether it be Hindu, Buddhist, or Taoist, the Mother represents vast space, wisdom beyond our comprehension, the plan of life beyond our conception, beyond form itself. Goddess Kali, in her highest and most radical aspect as these poems envision her, represents the Divine encompassing both male and female, appearing as female because this is a form that can answer our heart's longing—meeting us directly in our human forms, protecting us, nurturing us, captivating us, and taking us beyond the seeming safety of the conventional world into a boundless, nondual mystery beyond words.

It takes but a small stretch of the imagination to apply Ramprasad's visions of Kali to our experiential reality and to see her dancing powerfully in the world today. It is comforting and important to remember that this beautiful, uncontainable, sword-wielding goddess, who destroys what needs to be destroyed, simultaneously nurtures what is real in us. In the ancient Bengali tantric tradition of which Ramprasad was an initiate, these poems were not seen as mere literary invention but as actual vessels of Divine energy transmitted by the Mother to the poet and, through him, to anyone who could receive it. Singing words like these is a spiritual practice which fills and aligns the singer with the power of Divine Reality. More than two hundred years after they were composed, Ramprasad's poems are still sung throughout Bengal by everyone from beggars and shopkeepers to yogis and saints, infusing the daily world with awareness of the Mother's grace. Lex Hixon, initiated through the Ramakrishna lineage into the same Goddess tradition, has not translated the poems word for word, image for image. Using the originals as a basis, it is rather as if he has become available to the same spirit of the Divine which sang through Ramprasad, giving us newly inspired versions of the same transmission, bringing the Mother's energy and wisdom into a form suited to our time, culture, and sensibility.

TERROR

O Kali of Mystery!
I long to hold your luminous power
in the subtle nerve channels near the spine
long enough to know you more intensely.

Yet your brilliant Goddess energy
dances with freedom and wild abandon.
How can I possibly contain you, even for an instant?

The terror one might feel in admitting this energy into oneself and actually making the leap into boundlessness, as well as a related terror associated with the female, needs to be addressed.

Recorded history has always been in the hands of men. To a large segment of society, this record has become the accepted measure of reality. Side by side, however, with the information that was recorded in the masculine mode, there is a nonlinear tradition which, though not validated by the conventional intellect, has always existed. In this tradition, the Divine is feminine. Similar to the concealed treasure texts, or *termas*, of Tibetan Buddhism, which are discovered at the moment in time when they can be of most use to humanity, much is becoming available to us now that reveals the great deception, or at least limitation, which recorded history has imposed on every area of our perception. Both male and female scholars are now unearthing, in every tradition around the world, memories of a powerful female Deity, both creator and destroyer, fearsome and nurturing, beautiful and limitless and black. Her names or the names of her priestesses— the Celtic Caillech, the Saxon Kale, the Irish Kelles, the Semitic Kalu, the Spanish Califia, the Finnish Kalma, the Christian/Gypsy Sara-Kali, the Greek Kalli—are often variations of Kali. As news and memory of her spread into the collective consciousness, the effect on both the male and female psyche is bound to be revolutionary. She is the key to a missing part of our being. She represents a force beyond polarity and beyond convention which resonates with a mystery of life that has long been suppressed—not only in our psyches but in the permissible manifestation of women in the world—that has made our experience of life unbalanced and incomplete.

Although women in our time have been actively tearing down the old stereotypes, exploring and rebuilding themselves psychically and psychologically, nothing in our culture really prepares us for

217

the complete freedom and outrageous imagery with which Mother Kali is portrayed. The image of Mother Kali, wild hair flowing free, cutting off the heads of limited ideas so human beings can discover and experience for themselves the inherent freedom within, is a vision both men and women can benefit from and use as a guide. In it, the seeming violence, negativity, and incomprehensibility of life in this world is personified as a beneficent, even delightful, dancing force, and the often painful process of growth, change, and movement is shown to be nothing more than the loving game of illusion the Mother of Consciousness plays with her children as she helps them shed the fetters of the false perspective they cling to so that they can dance in freedom, too.

> *O Mother of the Universe,*
> *this child is terrified by your naked truth,*
> *your unthinkable blackness, your sheer infinity.*
> *Please cover your reality with a gentle veil.*

Terror. If we are to allow these poems to be Mother's living actions in the world—and I believe one of her gifts to us is to show us the way to stop separating the lofty inspiration of literature and the wisdom and beauty of sacred teachings from our everyday lives—we have to look at what prevents us from embracing them with our whole beings. I want to speak personally here, trusting that I don't speak for myself only.

Though since childhood I knew I was born to write, though the path of feminine spirituality has come very naturally to me, deeply imbedded in me are images I was brought up with which have censored me every step of the way. Though I never doubted creativity was an important part of my birthright, the models of those who were creative and powerful were male—everyone from the great artists and writers and composers, to God. The image of woman I unconsciously accepted, if she were not receptive and sweet and nurturing, was of a dangerous power whose beauty led to man's destruction—from Eve, ruining the Garden of Eden for Adam by choosing to eat from the tree of the knowledge of polarities rather than from the tree of life, to the nineteenth-century phantom ladies whose power was intoxicating and fatal—"La Belle Dame Sans Merci hath thee in thrall." And then there were those whose power and vision led to their own destruction—from Cassandra of Troy, whose vision of truth was not accepted and whose words were not believed, to twentieth-century women like Virginia Woolf or the poets Sylvia Plath and Anne Sexton, whose glimpses of that unbridled power was enough to drive them to madness and, finally, to suicide. There is no image in Western imagination of the strong woman whose contact with her primal power and wrathful quality of wisdom is welcomed and actually nurtures us. As for myself, always inside me there has been the presence of this power, but when I've felt it flow through me in more than a self-indulgent way, swung some metaphorical swords, and symbolically cut off some heads, the people in my life were seldom appreciative.

To find a beautiful goddess who is the very power of truth and the universe herself, sung of with love and devotion, worshiped and admired with reverence, who acts with this kind of fierceness on a grand scale is an inspiring relief. On the one hand, these poems give me joyous permission to nurture that part of myself in conjunction with my greater being. But on the other, the process of writing this essay has often brought me to a feeling of complete powerlessness and despair. How many times have I seen, in my own life and the lives around me, the very men who imagine that they worship and celebrate the qualities of truth and wisdom, wrath and wildness in a goddess, run from or invalidate the woman in their lives who displays them? How many men, face to face with a woman embodying her feminine power, can surrender their need to dominate, judge, or escape, and allow her, as the poet does, as Shiva does, to show them and give them the gift of her being, which is their being too?

In Hindu cosmology, this present era is called the *Kali Yuga*, the age in which Kali dances through the world in her wrathful, cleansing aspect, to be followed by the *Satya Yuga*, the Age of Truth. This movement from *Kali Yuga* to *Satya Yuga* must first be experienced within the life of each individual before the transition will take place globally. Our recorded history is a long story of male and female forces in disharmony. The poems in this book present us with a model of female as embodiment of infinitely wild wisdom, intensity, and creativity, and of male, as both poet and highest Deity, accepting and honoring her as such. This is quite a different dynamic than the one most men and women live out with each other. Does it have any validity, any bearing on the answers we seek at the end of this so-called Kali Age?

The Call to Freedom

The realms of being that you separate habitually,
calling them heaven and earth, divinity and humanity,
are simply forms of one universal Mother.

She manifests as eternal Goddess,
etheric beings, and earthly women.

These poems have encoded within them important information and initiatory energy for our time. Their images of the Supreme Feminine will no doubt be attractive to many men. Meeting the feminine as Goddess or Mother will enable men to understand and accept the feminine force in a new way, both as lofty, all-powerful Divine and also as the same force that runs through the women in their day-to-day existence. Women will recognize and identify with descriptions of the beautiful, dark Goddess in a way that men will not and feel awakened in them a longing and aspiration to fully embody this energy and have it loved and accepted.

However, men need to understand that the woman who gives herself to embody the Goddess is not always going to look like some beautiful image of the Divine Mother—sometimes, as she takes this energy into her own dark places and into the dark places of creation, she's going to look like what he wants to run away from. If at that time the man feels the terror Goddess Kali inspires and needs to tremble and quake to allow the woman to truly embody this power, these poems offer guidance in how to do that in an enlightened, noble fashion. Men must learn, despite the terror involved, how to empower and encourage women to step into their fullest being. The woman who allows this Kali energy and wisdom to flow through her will ultimately empower the men in her life, empower her sisters, and empower the world.

> *This avid worshiper of Mother is shocked*
> *that even supremely wise Lord Shiva*
> *cannot realize Kali's true nature.*

> *O supremely foolish poet,*
> *how can you hope to grasp her dancing feet*
> *that elude even Shiva's comprehension?*

To embrace Goddess energy and wisdom and let it mother us, dance in us, and free us is something we all, male and female, must do. As we welcome her energy within us, other, even more unexpected and surprising images of her than the ones in these poems, specific to the details of our lives and sensibilities, may come to us. It is important, as men and women, watching her in ourselves and each other, that we accept her unconditionally. To offer into her blazing light any personal sense of duality that her dancing energy within us reveals—whether experienced as judgment, censure, rigidity, or fear—is what she really asks of us, and is the most precious gift we can give her.

Recently, she instructed me in this way:

The Mother of the Universe
refuses to let me worship her outside myself anymore.
She has withdrawn inside me
and tells me if I want to know her
I have to come inside too, which is the last place I want to be.

221

Although she's been telling me this for years,
she's never gone to this extreme before
of actually hiding inside me.
If I want to love her,
I can only do it by loving myself now.
Oh, no!

Just as I used to walk around my room
offering incense, candlelight, and my being
to images of her,
she is now walking around inside me,
holding up a candle,
as if making her way through a dusty museum
or haunted house,
peering at the complex of my emotions
and distressing memories.
    It's time for you to clean house,
she tells me,
blowing the dust and cobwebs
off portraits of my relatives hung in the genes of my cells,
and scenes of past discomfort
hung in the long hallways of my body,
    clear out the space inside you
    until nothing remains but me.

    And I will then shine through you
    so that your true friends no longer have to be only the invisible ones
    whom you enshrined in your house,
    and worshiped for lack of trustworthy companionship.
    I will activate through you
    the love in them
    so you no longer have anything to fear
    from the hands and hearts of people in the world.

Jai Ma Kali! Om Sri Kali Ma!
May she dance in us, and may we learn to dance with her.